REASONABLE DOUBT
The Case for the UDR Four

To Peter Brooke
Secretary of State

With best wishes

from

Ian Paisley Jr.

REASONABLE DOUBT

The Case for the UDR Four

Ian Paisley, Jnr

Foreword
by
Robert Kee

THE MERCIER PRESS

THE MERCIER PRESS, 4 Bridge Street, Cork
24 Lower Abbey Street, Dublin 1

(c) Ian Paisley

ISBN 0 85342 962 6

A CIP record for this book is available from the British
Library.

Printed by Colour Books Ltd.

To Fiona

Contents

Acknowledgements

While writing this book I have received kindness and encouragement from many. It is fitting that I extend my gratitude and appreciation for their patience and understanding. Coming from a close family it is them I thank most for their practical help. The original idea came from my dad who introduced me to the case while working for him. As an employer he has been most understanding and flexible, permitting me to use his time to prepare parts of the manuscript. As a father he has been generous with advice and guidance. My mum has also been involved. She read the original drafts with much horror, and sometimes delight, and corrected the many grammatical pitfalls. It goes without saying how much I appreciate her help. And to my sister Cherith, who assisted with the preparation of the typed version I am deeply indebted.

It is necessary to thank the four families involved, especially Norman Bell for his untiring efforts to keep me up-to-date with the campaign. Other people have been most helpful in very practical terms. The staff at the Linenhall Library, Pacemaker International, Peter Robinson, MP, David Trimble MP, Barry Cowan, who acted as a sounding board for ideas and was a constant source of advice. The four solicitors, Messrs John Taylor, Joe Rice, John Cavanagh, Ted Jones and, Latimer's QC, Tony Cinnamond have all given generously of their time to assist with this enquiry. I would like to have been able to thank the RUC for their help. Regrettably however, any information I received from them was unofficial. The chief of the crime squad would not grant me an interview for the purpose of the book. That I very much regret.

It goes without saying, the thanks due to the four men who gave me permission to write this account of their story. That, I count as a privilege.

Foreword

ROBERT KEE

In recommending to anyone who is concerned for truth and justice this passionately argued book I have to declare an interest. Long before reading it I had become convinced, without any acquaintance with Ian Paisley Junior, that the four young men of the Ulster Defence Regiment he has written about here were innocent of the crime for which they have now been held in jails in Northern Ireland for over seven years.

But as a judge might say, addressing a jury in a normal British court, I must ask you to put that consideration out of your minds. For you, the readers, are in fact in the strange position of being the first jury ever to hear this case.

There are those who believe that the case of the Armagh Four was decided as long ago as 1983 soon after they were arrested. But it was only officially decided in 1986 and then, according to the due processes of law applying in Northern Ireland, by a single judge acting alone. Such a judge is of course in a somewhat invidious position. He has to sum up all the evidence in an objective and unbiased way while at the same time leading to a view or verdict that is positively biased in favour of guilt or innocence. He has in fact already come to a conclusion while publicly attempting to demonstrate his detachment from it. My own role here is easier.

It is simply to introduce a man who wishes to put a strong case to a jury. He is content that a jury should decide. And, in once again reminding you, members of the jury, that it is for you, not me, to make up your own minds. I should say that in doing so you must not fear if necessary to challenge the might of the British legal establishment.

The British legal establishment is firmly of the opinion that the judge who decided the Armagh Four case was right. In fact, the three judges who heard the case again in the Appeal Court found his judgment impeccable. But what is at stake here is something much more important than the opinion or reputation of judges: justice itself, which is finally not in the care of judges at all but of public opinion as represented in Britain's parliament.

Already a number of voices have been raised to question the legal establishment's certainty that the verdicts in this case are 'safe and satisfactory'. These include prominent Churchmen of the Methodist and Presbyterian Churches and the Protestant Archbishop of Armagh. The former Roman Catholic Archbishop of All Ireland, Cardinal Tomás Ó Fiaich, had made contact with the families of the convicted men before his tragic death in 1990. Among prominent Northern Ireland politicians to come to the conclusion that the verdicts were unsound was the late Harold McCusker, respected by all parties in Ireland except perhaps on the violent Orange Right. His wife, Jennifer, has been carrying on his campaign for a retrial. A former British Home Secretary, Merlyn Rees, a member of that delegation headed by Cardinal Hume which helped secure the release of the Guildford Four, has called for an enquiry. The Chief Constable of the RUC himself has decided that an enquiry of some sort, to be conducted admittedly only by a member of his own police force, is necessary.

But in the meantime, four young men — whom incidentally I have got to know personally by visiting them in prison and have been able to assess far more fully than any judge could possibly have done in court, though you must of course disregard that observation — have just spent their eighth Christmas in prison because the Secretary of State for Northern Ireland does not see fit to use his statutory powers to have the case reviewed. Hence Mr Paisley's passion. This may at times employ the technique of massive bombardment in preference to cautiously selective targeting but it is, in my view, all the more effective for that. Passion is what is needed here. For he presents a miscarriage of justice on a scale suffered by the Guildford Four, the Maguire household and the Birmingham Six.

Now Mr Ian Paisley Junior is of course, at least by association, a politician and a Unionist politician, like others who have shown public concern for the fate of the Armagh Four. It could be said that it is obviously in the interest of Unionist politicians to stand up for men of the Ulster Defence Regiment in their fight against the IRA. But this leaves out of account the fact that in this case they have to cast awkwardly critical reflections on the RUC who also fight the IRA. To have to do this has been a painful responsibility, as the late Harold McCusker and others have made clear, but they have rightly seen their duty as being primarily to that cause of British justice which both the UDR and the RUC are theoretically there to defend. It is an impressive aspect of Mr Paisley's book that he has maintained throughout this proper political detachment. His use of the judgment in another miscarriage of justice case, technically at the other end of the political spectrum — namely that of the Guildford Four — is one small example of this. But it is the spirit in which he has approached the case throughout, concerned only with the issue of right or wrong, justice or injustice, which serves as a model to anyone, whatever their political sympathies, who looks at the case of the Armagh Four.

It might seem tempting to some of a different political persuasion from Mr Paisley to think the Armagh Four guilty of the murder of the Catholic workman Adrian Carroll just because they sincerely think that the continued existence of the UDR is wrong and that such guilt usefully discredits it. Such thinking only discredits the cause of those who think this way. There is of course a perfectly rational argument to be made in favour of disbanding the UDR. There is also a perfectly rational case to be made for maintaining it. Neither of these arguments has anything to do with the case of the Armagh Four. That case, now, is simply about whether it can be said that the verdicts in the case against Neil Latimer, Noel Bell, James Hegan and Winston Allen were safe and satisfactory. Over to you, members of the jury.

Oh, and just by way of postscript, pay particular attention, would you, to two points: the possibility that while Witness A and Fr Faul were both sincerely expressing what they saw as the truth, the truth may have lain elsewhere, and the strange matter of the man who, the courts maintain, was responsible for the whole plot to murder Carroll and whose name and whereabouts they know, but against whom they have no evidence at all.

But don't of course on the other hand let yourself be influenced by anything I say. Just read Mr Paisley's book and cry to heaven and the British Secretary of State against miscarriages of justice.

ROBERT KEE

Introduction

While researching and writing this book I have been struck by the enigmatic paradox surrounding the peculiar circumstances of this case. A paradox, because here four men, Latimer, Bell, Hegan and Allen, were part of an institution and organisation lambasted for being Protestant and British by those who claim that the UDR is the whip that beats the Nationalists into submission. That organisation, the UDR, is one of the many facets that makes up the British system in Northern Ireland, it is in effect part of the establishment. Ten years ago no one would have believed that that same system could turn upon its own components. It has only been possible because the UDR has been bastardised continuously since its inception – even by other parts of the same establishment.

These men have been caught between the devil and the deep blue sea. On the one hand they are Protestant, British and ex-soldiers who were part of the British way of life in Ulster. They detested the ideas of those who challenged the Northern Ireland system, accepting that the police, army and courts were doing a job that had to be done. On the other hand they are now precariously placed out on a limb, claiming that they were wrongly convicted by the system they supported.

The purpose of my endeavours has been not to blacken the name of the Northern Ireland courts, judiciary or the gallant members of the Northern Ireland security services, whether they be members of the RUC or UDR, but rather to enquire after the truth and hopefully show that justice is universal. On that same reasoning I hope to show that an injustice of these gross proportions can happen to members of the Protestant and British community in Ulster as to Nationalists who have claimed it has happened to them.

Many ponderables remain unanswered. I have in no way attempted to blame any particular individual for this gross injustice. In strict legal terms I am convinced that the thesis of conviction was unsafe and have revised and excavated doubts which I believe support that claim. If these men have been convicted unfairly, then who is to blame?

In a way, I would argue, we all have to accept a portion of the burden. The courts backed an erroneous viewpoint that members of Her Majesty's forces deliberately, and with premeditation, set about to murder Adrian Carroll because of his political convictions. The general public were divided. Some accepted the proposition which the prosecution offered because they always believed the UDR were a danger to the precariously balanced peace in Northern Ireland and are in effect the regiment's enemies. Others believed that their own people had taken too much of the IRA's terrorism and sought revenge.

The sad fact is that another man has lost his life in this revengeful province, and members of a terrorist organisation which claims that murder, have walked free, leaving innocents to be jailed.

My purpose has not been to produce the actual gunman and hold him before the public claiming, 'He did it'. It is the duty of the police and courts to gather evidence and convict fairly. My purpose has been to examine this case and highlight the *reasonable doubts* therein. In doing so I am convinced that these men are innocent of the crime they have been incarcerated for and I believe there has been a mutilation of justice.

IAN R.K. PAISLEY, Jnr,
Belfast

1

Who Killed Adrian Carroll?

On a damp afternoon at approximately 4.30 on 8 November 1983, three gunshots echoed across an Armagh street, adding another name to the long list of victims of violence, and increasing the quota of grief in Northern Ireland. Adrian Carroll, a member of a Republican family, whose older brother, Roddy, an active service INLA member, was killed in a police counter-terrorist attack in South Armagh one year previously, met his death walking home from work as a painter at McCrum's Court on council premises. Adrian Carroll, aged 24, lived in a cul-de-sac off Abbey Street, in the centre of Armagh. As he walked home that November afternoon he was stalked by a lone gunman who approached him and shot him three times. One bullet entered his head, probably the fatal shot, the second his neck and the third his shoulder and chest. The weapon used for this cold blooded assassination was a .38 Smith and Wesson. Carroll struggled to live but the extent of his injuries claimed his life and he was pronounced dead at 7.30 that evening.

Adrian Carroll, it appeared, became another victim of a spiral of sectarian killings that have crippled both communities in Northern Ireland for more than twenty years. Hours after his death a statement released to a Belfast press agency claimed that the murder was carried out by the Protestant Action Force, a label of convenience used by the infamous Ulster Volunteer Force. Originally set up as a vigilante counter-terrorist organisation it plummeted into a sectarian murder machine in a senseless attempt to fight Republican terrorism with Loyalist reprisal, and in effect added to the violence and misery of the province.

In a statement the PAF claimed they had shot Adrian Carroll because he was a Republican. This claim appeared to point to the inevitable – that the sectarian killings would continue and Carroll would be a number in the body count of Northern Ireland's political war. Surprisingly police investigations did not lead to arrests or charges of PAF suspects in Belfast or Armagh, but rather a bewildering and astonishing episode of events, arrests and eventual trial of members of the security forces took place.

Although four men – Neil Latimer, James Hegan, Noel Bell and Winston Allen – have all been convicted of murder, aiding and abetting murder and assisting in the murder of Adrian Carroll, a strange sense of 'unfinished work' has surrounded the verdict. The Protestant Action Force, consistently and for no apparent reason, overstepped the usual boundary of their seclusion, insisting that not one of the accused or anyone associated with them took part in this act of violence. The organisation that perpetrated this action maintains that the murderer is free. If an organisation goes to these unprecedented lengths to claim a murder, the suspicions of all must be alerted.

When the question *Who killed Adrian Carroll?* arises, it opens a kaleidoscopic inquiry on the issue of justice, not only for Carroll that his murderer be found and convicted, but also for Latimer, Hegan, Bell, Allen and their other colleagues implicated, that their names be cleared of a murder they say they did not commit. Carroll's death and the ensuing enquiry that led to the conviction of four UDR soldiers for his murder raise questions that the pillars supporting the workings of our society, the judiciary, the police and to an extent the politicians, must face and answer. Never has so much doubt concerning a conviction in Northern Ireland vocalised itself like this one. 'British Injustice' – a slogan of retribution, has been hurled at convictions outside Northern Ireland. No one will forget the campaign sighting the miscarriage of justice in England surrounding the Guildford Four and the spin-off effect this had on the Maguire convictions and the Birmingham Six. While the UDR Four is in no way to be seen as the 'Guildford Four in drag' – there are many differences between the two cases – the reliability of police notes taken contemporaneously during interviews with suspects is at issue, and was disputed by the UDR Four at their trial.

The extensive area of justice, and for that matter injustice, must be examined carefully and reimposed on what actually happened in Armagh on 8 November 1983. During December of that year a series of arrests of members of the security forces took place. Three of the men were tried and convicted of murder on the basis of uncorroborated statements made while in the custody of the RUC at Castlereagh Holding Centre. The UDR Four were convicted of murder after a sixty-eight day trial at Belfast Crown Court. Throughout their trial they persistently made the claim that the police had used unfair and repressive methods in questioning them. This, they allege, led them to make statements incriminating themselves. The statements, they say, were not voluntary. The mechanisms of justice in any democracy must be open to scrutiny. This is a matter of public interest. The RUC denied the claims made by the four men. The judge, after carefully examining the evidence, decided the police were telling the truth and the UDR Four were lying. However, if the contemporaneous evidence which resulted from their investigations is questionable, no matter how insignificant or peripheral, and this can be upheld, then the question *Who shot Adrian Carroll?* must be reassessed. Neil Latimer, Noel Bell, James Hegan and Winston Allen must be retried as they have consistently demanded since their convictions in July 1986.

The UDR Four case does not stop with these four men. Others were implicated in this trial, and in Lord Justice Kelly's phrase the 'audacious murder' penetrated deeper than the convictions suggest. Altogether thirteen UDR soldiers, a fourteenth guard, and the entire credibility of the regiment were soiled by the trial.

An unrelenting campaign to discredit the Ulster Defence Regiment has been the political desire and primary activity of several people in Northern Ireland. This trial presented such like minded people with the ammunition and opportunity to slander and blame the Ulster Defence Regiment for political murder. It is ironic that the police achieved credibility among their critics and the enemies of the regiment – to the detriment of that force. In effect the trial of the UDR Four became a trial for the hearts and minds of a hostile public, of the credibility of the UDR as opposed to the professionalism of the RUC.

Accusations of this nature, made by the UDR at the trial, tug at the heart-strings of anyone who believes that the system is correct and that the checks and balances are adequate. The subsequent fall-out from the trial has dented the system. Those who are concerned with fairness and impartiality must be prepared to take note and allow the pillars of our society go through the same rigorous investigations as we allow other individuals to go through. If the convictions are safe the police and courts have nothing to fear as they shall emerge unsoiled. If a genuine mistake was made, then the mistake must be rectified, and if a miscarriage of justice has occurred, those responsible must be held accountable and the men who have suffered as a result must be allowed demonstrate and prove their innocence. If Latimer, Bell, Hegan and Allen are not guilty — who then killed Adrian Carroll?

2

The Accused

Maghaberry prison is set in the tranquil area of South
Antrim overlooking the Lagan Valley and close to the
flower filled, award winning village of Moira in County
Down. On approaching the prison, through the picturesque
surrounding countryside, one is suddenly struck by the
concrete, fortified imposition in what appears to be the
middle of nowhere. Maghaberry like all prisons in
Northern Ireland, is top security. Yet its regime is not as
militarised as that of HMP Maze, which continues to
maintain its paramilitary air. Billed as a modern prison,
with a friendly yet strict atmosphere, the inmates serve
time knowing that out of all the prisons in Northern
Ireland and the United Kingdom, Maghaberry is probably
the most modern and the most comfortable – if that latter
term can be applied!

It is not a glamorous place to visit. Prison visits are a
great leveller. On my first visit to Maghaberry to see
prisoner number A1143 Winston Allen, it struck me that
despite the reassurances from prison staff and the authorities that Maghaberry is the best prison in Northern
Ireland, I still got a chilling sense of indignity and loss of
personal freedom – windows, subtly blackened to prevent
curious and prying eyes stealing a glimpse of sensitive and
secure areas, body searches, van rides and door after door
along secure passages to the visitors' wing.

Before going to Maghaberry I was aware that there was
widespread unease with the convictions of Neil Latimer,

19

Noel Bell, James Hegan and Winston Allen. Serious doubts concerning the nature of the evidence and the thesis upon which they were convicted had been called into question by politicians and opinion formers across the board. Peter Brooke, the Secretary of State for Northern Ireland, who has demonstrated himself more capable of listening than his predecessor, stated in parliament and in a written answer to parliamentary questions that he would be prepared to consider a retrial of the UDR Four case if he could be presented with fresh factors and new evidence. The families of the convicted men were adamant that they had found flaws in the convictions. They brought their concerns to several Unionist politicians including party leaders Ian Paisley and James Molyneaux; deputy leaders, including the late Harold McCusker (who said before his death that he wished to see these men, who he believed were innocent, freed), Peter Robinson and Ken Maginnis – to churchmen including the late Cardinal Tomás Ó Fiaich, the Presbyterian Moderator Dr Mathews and the past Methodist chairman Rev. Hamilton Skillen, and to the eminent historian and broadcaster Robert Kee. I was therefore aware that the verdict of Lord Justice Basil Kelly, and the subsequent verdict of the three appeal judges, was considered unsafe by many and I was eager to learn more by putting faces and personalities to the names and data I had already studied.

Accusations arising from a theory that a few senior ranking RUC men framed the Four have resulted in libel writs being issued on the BBC, Barry Cowan and the historian Robert Kee. No such suggestion is made here. The purpose of this book is not to allege any impropriety on the part of any members of the RUC investigation team.

The UDR Four are asserting they are innocent. This book seeks to examine their claims in the light of what transpired at their trial. Certainly a study of the trial transcript shows that they did make allegations of impropriety against certain members of the RUC. These were carefully considered by the trial judge. He rejected their claims.

The purpose of this book is to examine if in all the circumstances the conviction is safe. The claims of the men and the counterclaims of the police are fairly and accurately set out as they were made at the men's trial. Part of the UDR Four's claims that they are innocent rests on their claim that they only made statements after they felt obliged to make them. As such they say the statements were not voluntary and should not have been tendered as evidence against them.

Neil Latimer is 5' 11", of slim build and dark complexion. As I sat at the interview table in Maghaberry prison with his mother and girlfriend waiting for him to arrive, I saw a jolly young man coming towards me. As Neil sat down, obviously aware I was visiting, he nodded, smiled and said: 'right there'.

Neil Fraser Latimer was born on 4 March 1962. He was the fourth son of Mr and Mrs Latimer and was resident in Armagh all his life. Latimer was described by Lord Justice Kelly as – 'being of average intelligence and quite sharp'. Latimer was educated at Armagh Secondary College and then Armagh Technical College. He did not excel in any particular field but he enjoyed art and physical pursuits. At seventeen he had enough of formal education and left school, taking on a position as apprentice butcher at Flannigan's in Armagh. He stayed with the butchery profession for one year then left for better money as a cutter at a shirt factory. Latimer soon found himself tired of the cutting and got employment at another factory. This was his first steady job and lasted for two and a half years until he was made redundant. It was while at this factory that Latimer met a middle-aged woman who six years later at his trial was to play a significant role in determining his future.

According to his mother, Neil 'got through life'.[1] He

was always in employment except for a short period of seven months before he joined the UDR. His main motive for joining was to get off the depressing 'dole'. Latimer was a happy-go-lucky young man and it was this quality, despite his current predicament, that shone through when I met him in Maghaberry.

On my questioning him concerning his experiences in November/December, 1983 Latimer talked openly and did not shy away from any accusations I insisted on raising concerning his involvement with paramilitaries; the allegation that he was guilty as charged; that the evidence against him amounted to an insurmountable brick wall that appeared impossible to break down — this included an eyewitness account that he had been seen by Witness A in Lonsdale Street shortly before the murder in civilian clothes and a silimar disguise was worn by the gunman as witnessed by Elaine Faulkner; that he was the first to sign a statement admitting guilt to the murder which ultimately led to his conviction. He was arrested on 29 November when he was taken directly to Castlereagh Holding Centre and not Gough barracks, as is the usual procedure when soldiers are questioned. His initial reaction was one of shock. After all, he was a serving member of the security forces invested with equal powers to arrest suspects. Latimer had little dealings with the police in his past or in his work. He told me that if only someone had taken him aside and told him about Castlereagh he would have been better prepared to undergo what was to follow. Obviously Latimer would be acquainted with certain police officers while on duty but nothing extensive. A certain distance was maintained, while on patrol, which was never overstepped. The RUC were colleagues in the broadest sense of the word, a kind of 'them' and 'us' attitude prevailed he said. Nonetheless they were all part of the same system sharing the same ultimate goals.

Latimer was initially shocked by the way he was treated. At first he did not recall his duties on 8 November

22

and insisted he had been on foot patrol the day Carroll was murdered. At the trial Latimer's defence argued that he was 'subjected to inordinate pressure and improprieties by the detectives at Castlereagh during his time there between the 29th November 1983 and the 6th December 1983'. In his judgment Lord Justice Kelly summarised Latimer's defence:

> Their questioning [the detectives] was persistent and aggressive. They shouted and bawled at him. They threatened that he would get a long jail sentence if he did not confess but that if he did, he would get out of Castlereagh on bail. He alleged no physical assault by any detectives but the ill-treatment he complained of was such that, to use his phrase, it 'scared the life out of him'. It made him worried, depressed and confused and left him with the resolve to do anything to get out of Castlereagh.
> The result was that he was induced to make false confessions to murder. He made no such confessions. What he told them and what they call his confessions was to use his phrases 'what they wanted to hear' in order to 'get them off his back'. The content of his alleged verbal and written confessions insofar as it involved him in the knowledge of or participation in the murder was completely false. It came from what the detectives had suggested to him, what they said the evidence against him was and partly also from his own inventions. In all the circumstances it was submitted that I should in the exercise of my discretion rule against their admissibility and find no confession came from him.[2]

The judge then turned his attention to the police claims and to the prosecution case:

> All his allegations of ill-treatment were denied by the detectives. They said that althoug (sic) he had denied involvement initially he verbally confessed to having shot Carroll at the third interview of the first day (4.05 p.m. – 7.05 pm, 29th November 1983) and later that evening (Interview No. 4 between 9.05 p.m. and 9.37 p.m.) he dictated and signed a written confession to the like effect (Exhibit No. 7).
> The essence of these confessions was that he carried out

the shooting on his own in civilian clothes but he was not prepared to name anyone else involved. The detectives put it to him the next day (the 30th November 1983) that other U.D.R. men were involved. He denied this and then retracted his confessions of the evening before. 'None of the patrol were involved. I didn't shoot the man' he said and what he had said before in Exhibit No. 7 was lies.

But then on the following day (1st December 1983) having in the morning denied that any of his U.D.R. comrades in the Land Rovers had stopped in Lonsdale Street or picked up a civilian there, he admitted in the afternoon that they had and did but he said he did not know the civilian. So the Crown say that he had moved at this stage from denying his fellow soldiers were involved to admitting that they were and from admitting that he was the gunman to saying someone else was. The 'someone else' whom he said he did not know became someone whose identity he did not want to reveal (Interview No. 14 7.00 p-m. – 8.40 p.m.)[3]

According to the crown Latimer went on building upon these confessions until eventually he told the whole truth. Latimer claims he was naive regarding police activities and procedure, that he broke down under such treatment and claims he confessed under pressure. He was agreeing with police suggestions until he felt his only way out of the bewildering circumstances was to sign a confession. These confessions I will examine in detail later.

In his judgment Lord Justice Kelly said:

I therefore saw a good eal (sic) of him [Latimer] in the witness box. He is I think of average intelligence and quite sharp. A vast amount of what the detectives say that he said to them was admitted by him as what he probably did say but he said it was all lies, at least any part that told or suggested that he was involved in the Carroll murder. He admitted therefore that he had confessed to having shot Carroll on the first day of interviewing and of having dictated the written statement of confession (Exhibit No. 7) that evening but all was a bundle of lies brought about by the state he had been reduced to and the desire to get out of Castlereagh ...

Latimer explained that what led him to the later phase of involving the U.D.R. in the murder but not himself as the

24

gunman came from the detectives' suggestion that if they were willing to accept he was not the gunman he must still know something about it as the driver of a Land Rover that day. He went along with this although it was not of course true. Again it came from the detectives that the gunman might have been someone who resembled him in appearance such as his brother David and eventually he went along with that one too.

When he confessed again that he was the gunman and his comrades were involved in the murder, this was made up by him from what the detectives had told him, some of it was his own invention or came from talk about the murder afterwards around the camp. And it was given by him because the conduct of the detectives had put him in such a state that he wanted to get out of Castlereagh and that he would have done anything to achieve that.

He said he would have named his own brother as the gunman to get himself out ...[4]

The trial judge dismissed Latimer's suggestions that the police were lying and he was truthful:

It became painfully obvious that Latimer was constantly lying. In re-examination he proclaimed he was good at inventing things. If this meant he was good at telling lies I would agree in part. Certainly he told lies to the detectives But I do not think he was good, meaning successful, at telling lies in court.[5]

The sentence spelled out lucidly the judge's decision that Latimer was guilty as charged. He went on to say:

I believe he [Latimer] was in full control of his situation at Castlereagh ... I believe Latimer was deeply conscious of the seriousness of his position. I believe the detectives underlined this by repeating, no doubt in a firm way, that they had strong information of his involvement and this led to his verbal admission he was the gunman ... I find it hard to believe that a soldier after only two interviews at which the sum of ill-treatment was nothing more than shouting, a threat and a promise of favour, would falsely confess to a murder and to the prime role in it ...[6]

> I have concluded that Latimer's confessions were freely and voluntarily made. Equally I am satisfied that they can be given full probative value and weight. I remind myself that I am considering the weight of the confessions of a young man, but an adult, of average intelligence and one who is not an idiot or a fool. But more than that. I am considering the weight of the confessions of a member of the Security Forces, a serving soldier in the Ulster Defence Regiment given to other members of the Security Forces, R.U.C. detectives ...[7]

The question why should someone who is innocent confess to something they did not do has been confronted by Dr Alexander Kellam, a consultant forensic psychiatrist for the South Glamorgan Health Authority, an acknowledged expert on this subject. An article by Simon Denison (talking to Dr Alexander Kellam) in the *Daily Telegraph*, 25 January 1989 – 'Why Innocent Cries Can Turn to Guilty Starts' – says 'Psychological proofs exist that quite ordinary people do what they are told by figures in authority, even when they mean not to'. Latimer's case is that he was obedient to authority. The fact that he was a soldier only emphasises the point. Unlike a terrorist he would not be conditioned to withstand police interrogation procedure.

Could it not equally be argued that the fact they were members of the security forces could have worked against them? One minute Latimer was on the streets with the full backing of the law, the next he was in Castlereagh, the tables turned, considered a criminal, a terrorist! Could it have been this volte-face that in his words confused his mind and broke him?

I put the question of his confessions to him. Why would he, knowing he was innocent, confess to the police? In reply Latimer raised the allegations he had made at his trial – which were not accepted by the trial judge:

> Castlereagh is a hostile place. Once you've been in there your whole life changes. I was unaware of what the hell they [the police] were going to say and do to me. They twisted my every word. As I said before now, if you had given me a gun I

26

would have shot myself, I would have done myself in – I was so scared and confused. Unless you've been in Castlereagh you will never understand how it really feels. Banging your head against a brick wall knowing you are innocent yet them proving you are guilty.[8]

Latimer said that he was bitter about the whole affair. He knows that as long as he protests the courts' decision and continues to claim innocence the prison authorities will not exercise leniency or discretion with his sentence.

James Hegan, senior to his colleagues by fifteen years, was a lance corporal in the UDR, an excellent marksman, intelligent and articulate. He struck me as a man desperate and eager to prove his innocence. I visited him with his wife, three children and his father, Tom Hegan. I was able to do more than empathise with the children's position of seeing their father in jail, being told he is innocent and then having to leave him there. I had once been in that position as a child.

Hegan was born on 19 April 1950 and educated at Newry High School. He lived in Newry until 1984 when his wife and family were intimidated out of their home. Hegan began his working days in a stitching and tie factory, and supplemented his earnings by part-time UDR work which he grew to love. In 1979 the opportunity presented itself to develop this part-time love into a full-time career. Unemployment was running high resulting in the closure of the factory where Hegan worked and he decided then to join the full-time UDR.

His passion for army life rewarded him with promotion to the position of lance corporal in D company. Hegan had an acknowledged skill with firearms, accompanying the UDR team to competitions as a top marksman. His home is arrayed with trophies and medals he won. He married his wife, Lillian, in 1971. She told me he was, 'dedicated to army life'. They have three children – Sharon (16), Gary

(12), and Arlene (8).

James Hegan is a straight-talking man. He spoke lucidly concerning his experience in Castlereagh Holding Centre. Hegan was arrested on Saturday 3 December 1983. According to the police he confessed to a knowledge of the murder on 6 December, and was charged and eventually convicted of aiding and abetting the murder of Adrian Carroll.

Hegan maintains that his mind became a toy from his experience. The allegations that the statements were improperly obtained were first considered in the 'trial within the trial' known as the *Voir Dire*. In an ordinary criminal trial this evidence is heard in the absence of the jury to prevent them from hearing prejudicial evidence which would be inadmissible. However, in this case there was no jury, rather the case was heard by a Diplock court. That is a court established from recommendations made in the Diplock report, 1972, wherein Lord Diplock recommended that for certain terrorist offences in Northern Ireland trials should be heard before judges sitting alone. The *Voir Dire* is used so that the judge must first hear the evidence wearing his judge's hat, during this he may hear evidence which he must decide is inadmissible. Later, having heard this evidence he must discount it when he comes to wearing his juror's hat.

Hegan claims he had weaknesses which ultimately broke him and led him to making a confession. The weaknesses were voiced by Hegan at the trial between 8 – 12 May 1986. In his judgment Lord Justice Kelly outlined Hegan's defence. He said:

> They said that he with others who had carried out the Carroll murder were indirectly responsible for the Darkley shootings. He was kept standing throughout the interview. It lasted for over three hours. The whole interview was a shouting match and it ended with Inspector [John] Brannigan threatening that he would have him standing ballock naked on the table and he would slap the legs off him.

He continued to protest his innocence at subsequent interviews on the 3rd and the 4th. He had been told earlier that Latimer and Bell had admitted their parts and parts of Latimer's and Bell's statements had been read to him. He could not understand how Latimer and Bell could be involved.

At interview No. 6 on the 4th December between 4.00 p.m. and 5.05 p.m. he encountered Detective Inspector [John] Brannigan and Detective Constable [Robert Alexander] Orr again. When they came into the interview room Brannigan shouted 'Stand up' and when he did Orr came to his front, put his hands round the back of his neck, pulled his head down and shook it and at the same time shouted questions in both his ears.

He was told he would get 30 years and that he would not be out of prison until the year 2013 and he was told what the ages of his children would be then. He stood throughout this interview. The records show that it lasted for one hour and five minutes.[9]

Hegan claimed that this treatment compounded the already mounting confusion he felt. Threats that he would serve thirty years left him desperate. 'A kind of brainwashing took place until I was ready to agree to the interrogators suggestions'.[10] No one could believe his innocence and he could not understand why. He claims he was told Latimer and Bell were turning queen's evidence. Physically he was weak and tired. The police, he said, told him that they were his friends. If he wanted out it would be better for him to make a statement distancing himself from the whole affair. Hegan claims he was tricked and confused into making the confessions. The police deny all improprieties. The judge accepted their view. In his judgment Lord Justice Kelly said:

Their notes [the police] told all or almost all. This combined with strong denials of impropriety makes it difficult for a tribunal of fact to invoke from demeanour where the truth may lie. Occasionally this is just possible and I had the impression that Detective Inspector [John] Brannigan and Detective Sergeant [William] Johnston at least appeared to be telling the truth.

And I do not think that Detective Inspector Brannigan would be so foolish to take part in or permit his colleague to take part in the physical abuse alleged before the television cameras of the interview room. There were of course discrepancies and some inconsistencies between the evidence of some of the pairs of detectives but on all important and central matters there was accord.

One looks very closely at the central evidence of the detective wherever any inconsistency appears even where peripheral. Again one must always remind oneself that the measured and quiet manner of the detective in the witness box and his careful voice does not reflect the reality of the interview room. I would be surprised if interviewing detectives did not raise their voices at times shout and be or appear to be aggressive or impatient. But with television cameras in the interview rooms now as they have been for some time and the monitoring of what goes on sensible detectives must be aware of the folly of physical ill-treatment or even keeping a suspect standing for periods.[11]

Hegan's account of events was obviously rejected by Lord Justice Kelly who said:

What destroyed Hegan's case on ill-treatment was not merely the consistent denial of it by the police detectives, in which I found no cause for disbelief, and not merely the implications of the medical evidence but the evidence and demeanour of Hegan himself.

He entered the witness box with some aplomb. He gave his evidence in chief in a quite impressive way. His manner and demeanour then was confident and authoritative. He expressed himself freely and lucidly. His recall of the events of the first twenty interviews appear to be long and meticulous. His formal academic education was no more and perhaps less than some of his co accused but he struck me as the most intelligent by far. A very astute man indeed. I can understand why he holds superior rank and I suspect that he was an efficient soldier.

But in a number of ways these qualities proved self defeating in the context of his case on admissibility. I would think that of all the accused, no one is more conscious than

Hegan of his membership of and standing in the Security Forces. No one is more aware of rules of discipline to which members of the security forces are subject and of the procedures that exist to maintain their enforcement. So I believe that no one of Hegan's calibre and situation would suffer the indignity and blatant breach of discipline that his alleged ill treatment brought about from as early as his second interview, without blatant and robust reaction.

It fits the man that when his involvement in the murder was shouted to him by the detectives that he shouted back his innocence. But it does not fit the man to be knocked about physically, to listen to threats to have his wife arrested, and his three young children taken into care under Derrybeg supervision, to be falsely accused of involvement in a murder, to be threatened with 30 years imprisonment for no reason without taking immediate steps and every possible step to end it and redress it.[12]

Noel Bell was the youngest of the platoon of UDR soldiers on duty the day Adrian Carroll was shot. The whole of the evidence against him is uncorroborated and based upon a confession made while in Castlereagh. Bell claims it was made under duress. At his trial Bell alleged that he was mistreated in a disgraceful manner.

Noel Bell is the second son of Mr and Mrs Norman Bell. Norman Bell has been the most vocal advocate of all the relatives advocating the innocence of the UDR Four. He has demonstrated his commitment, being prepared to go anywhere and speak to anyone in an effort to publicise the plight of the UDR Four. Mr Bell led the families in a delegation to see the late Cardinal Tomás Ó Fiaich requesting that he examine the roles played by the priests involved, Denis Faul and Raymond Murray.

Noel Bell left school in order to take up an apprenticeship with Dukes' Transport. He had a keen interest in mechanics and was sponsored by his employers to Felton House for his City and Guilds. He was awarded 'Northern Ireland Apprentice of the Year' for exemplary work. In 1983 Noel Bell left Dukes and joined the full-time UDR. Bell had an unhappy childhood and found that his only comfort seemed to be alcohol. He had lost his driver's licence the year before joining the UDR because of a drink-driving charge. This was the only brush he had with the law. Noel Bell served as a full-time soldier until his arrest in 1983.

Bell was arrested at four o'clock in the morning of 2 December. He was suffering from a hangover as he was still a heavy drinker. He was taken directly to Castlereagh. It emerged during his trial that he had attempted suicide on four occasions. Medical specialists at his trial claimed that he was easy prey for his interrogators due to his hangover, and an inability to withstand sustained pressure. Dr Lindy Burton, a consultant psychologist, gave evidence claiming that she had interviewed Noel Bell on 5 September 1984 at Crumlin Road Prison. At the trial on 8 April 1986 Dr Burton said that when she examined Bell she gave him a 16 personality factor questionnaire. She said:

> He was slightly nervous, my lord, and throughout my rexamination *(sic)* he tended to sweat profusely but initially he stuttered and appeared somewhat diffident ...
>
> The 16 personality factor questionnaire ... is a most rigorous and objective personality test, the most rigorous and objective that is available to us ... There appeared to be no indications of underlying neurological abnormality. There appeared to be some indications of psychological disturbance in the realm of anxiety and mild depression but on the objective personality test of the 16 p.f. 13 factors were non nomral *(sic)* ...
>
> The picture presented by this measure was one of a very unstable young man who tended to fly away from problems rather than fight them. He tended not to face them: tended to run away from them and was extremely submissive, timid and extremely naive. He had a high level of anxiety on this measure and he appeared unable to control this anxiety ...
>
> He said he had been a very unhappy child. He had tended to run away a great deal. He was often in trouble both at home and at school. He was a third child of a family of four. He felt that the other children got more attention than he got .... He was unhappy at school. He felt that he was picked upon

.... During his teens he made four separate attempts on his onw (sic) life. The first attempt was made when he was 14 years, when he consumed a considerable dose of anadin. The next attempt was when he was 15 when he mixed tablets and took these and then when he was 18 or 19 when he tried to kill himself by locking himself in his garage running his car and lying in the carbon monoxide fumes. On Christmas morning of 1982 when he was 19 he did this and in addition made usre (sic) that he took a lot of tablets which he hoped was going to end his life ...

From the age of 13 he began to take alcohol whenever he could obtain it. At 16 he was sent to Felden House to train and he was living away from home. He consumed as much alcohol as he could get his hands on ...

He seemed a very vulnerable young man, my lord, one who obviously had major emotional problems. He seemed very unsettled and very unsure of himself and with a very strong feeling that his life was not really very important to anyone. I think because of this he felt depressed.[13]

Such a record highlighted the failure of the UDR to vet recruits adequately. His father and mother hoped that the discipline of the regiment would steady their vulnerable son.

At his trial Bell gave evidence that he was verbally and physically abused by the detectives. He recounts that although feeling groggy he remembers becoming, 'frightened and scared' because of their attitude and conduct.[14] Bell was interviewed six times during the first day of his detention. He was not permitted to smoke and claims the detectives continuously shouted him down on each occasion when he claimed he was innocent.

During a *Voir Dire* to determine the admissibility of police evidence, Bell accused Det. Sgt Thomas Clements and Det. Con. John Shiels of attacking him because he would not admit guilt.[15] He claimed he was punched in the chest, slapped in the face and punched in the testicles twice and he fell to the ground.[16] Bell said he was scared and felt he had no choice but to co-operate with the police or else the beatings would continue. He remembers Chief

Supt James Mitchell being brought into the room and 'he said something like "I am glad that you have seen sense."'[17] Bell claimed he was told that he would get home that evening if he co-operated, and on this promise he gave in.[18] He was depressed, exhausted and beaten. Bell was dependent upon alcohol as Dr Burton stated, and when pressure was applied he claims he took the line of least resistance.

On 18 March 1986 during a *Voir Dire* Bell recounted his experience at Castlereagh:

> I was really frightened, my lord. I did not know what was going to happen and none of these boys were going to believe me and I just could not take any more of it. I was going to have to get them off my back.
>
> Q: And what was your physical condition at this time?
>
> A: I was exhausted, my lord. I just could not take any more of it.
>
> Q: And did Detective Sergeant [Thomas] Clements get the chief?
>
> A: He left the room, my lord, and came back again within two minutes.
>
> Q: And who was the chief? ...
>
> A: He came back with Detective Superintendent [James] Mitchell, my lord.
>
> Q: And did he say something to you?
>
> A: Yes, my lord.
>
> Q: What did he say to you?
>
> A: He said something like, 'I am glad to see that you have seen sense', my lord.[19]

The crown case against Bell pointed to a rather different story. According to the prosecution he was told by his UDR accomplices that there was going to be a shooting. Bell had a particular role to play — he was to assist with the mock-arrest of Latimer at Armagh Technical College in Lonsdale Street. Accordingly, Bell assisted with the arrest and waited in the landrover while Latimer did the shooting. To prove this the crown relied upon Bell's confession at Castle-reagh Holding Centre. Although its admissibility was

challenged on the grounds that it was induced by inhuman
or degrading ill-treatment, Lord Justice Kelly found that it
was admissible. In his judgment he said: 'I found the crown
evidence had satisfied me beyond reasonable doubt that
Bell was not ill-treated as he alleged'.[20]

In his judgment Lord Justice Kelly gave eleven reasons
why he did not accept Bell's account of events at Castlereagh. These included:

> It seemed highly unlikely in this case that the detectives
> would indulge in physical ill-treatment of the nature and
> degree claimed by Bell when television cameras were
> operating ...
> Bell's alcoholic dependence and deprivation did not
> appear, from Bell's own evidence, to have been a significant
> factor in the making of the statement ...
> I think it is necessary to remember throughout when one
> is considering the detail of this issue, that one is here con-
> cerned with a serving soldier of average intelligence,
> accustomed to associating with the RUC, at least the uni-
> formed side, and to hwom (sic) a police station (or a holding
> centre) is not the strange or forbidding place it may be to
> other suspects. Further, his questioning and the statement he
> signed related to guilty involvement in the serious charge of
> murder. With this in mind very many adverse comments on
> Bell's context on admissibility can be mooted. It leads,
> among other questions, to ask why after the first assault he
> did not demand to see a senior police officer and complain;
> why after the vicious violence from Detective Sergeant
> [Thomas] Clements in the sixth interview he didnt (sic)
> protest to Detective Chief Superintendent [James] Mitchell
> who entered the room immediately following it and why he
> did not complain to some one detective or policeman the
> whole time at Castlereagh ... To submit to these improprieties
> without complaint, to acquiesce to a concocted confession to
> murder, to make things up to add to that confession just to
> please the police seems unbelievable conduct by a member
> of the Security Forces ...[21]

Bell's excuse that he would not trust anyone in Castlereagh
to complain to were found to be unacceptable. Lord Justice

Kelly said: 'I find it impossible to accept such a person would accept ill-treatment without robust protest and complaint'.[22] On the issue of the frame up of Bell and his colleagues Lord Justice Kelly found the idea unacceptable as: 'I do not understand why any detective, including a Detective Chief Superintendent, would want to frame him and concoct against him a confession to murder. Why him? Did the detectives want to discredit the UDR?'[23]

The last to be convicted of Carroll's murder was *Winston Allen* – a most unlikely would-be murderer. Allen was twenty-two when Carroll was murdered. He was convicted of the murder of Adrian Carroll and of carrying out the instructions of a fifth man, Sergeant Roleston. Sergeant Walter Roleston was never charged or convicted of any crime. He had a long-standing service record with the UDR until shortly after the trial when his service was not renewed. The implausibility of the crown scenario is emphasised to its ultimate folly when one considers that in Allen's confession he names Walter Roleston as the man on the spot who gave the orders on how the murder plan should be executed. Not only was he named as the mastermind behind the plot in Allen's statement but his credibility as a law-abiding UDR officer was soiled when, Lord Justice Kelly said in his judgment, the crown alleged:

> Near the end of the second search, the first stage of the murder plan was put into operation. This involved the accused Private Allen driving a Land Rover away from the search into the city with the accused Private Latimer who was to be the gunman and Sergeant Rolston *(sic)*, not before the court, on board. They drove to Lonsdale Street, stopped and left Latimer off at the Technical College ... The Land Rover with Allen and the sergeant returned to the Moy Road search.[24]

Sgt Roleston has always denied any involvement in the murder of Adrian Carroll. Yet his colleagues were convicted on the basis he was the senior army officer organising the murder of Adrian Carroll.

Winston Allen, a devout Christian who was in regular attendance at 'The Cleft' (a religious gathering for young people held in Portadown), joined the full-time Ulster Defence Regiment in April 1983 after three years part-time service. Allen joined in an effort to supplement his income from the family farm in Loughgall. He had only moved to D company five days prior to Carroll's murder. If the crown scenario is to be believed he was brought into the murder plan as an unknown quantity. He was not from the Armagh area but from Richhill. He was more familiar with Portadown, yet in his statements he is supposed to have recounted place-names in a familiar way which he and his family say he just would not have known. His family say this casts doubt on the veracity of his statement. Allen was a fish out of water, never a typical soldier. His colleagues considered him to be quiet and shy. Allen did not even know all the men on the patrol that day due to his recent transfer, and they in turn would not have known him. Was this sufficient reason to bring him into the murder plot? The crown wishes us to accept that this unlikely man was one of the conspirators who planned and assisted in the Carroll murder. Who in their right mind would involve an unknown quantity in a murder plan? The judge called the murder plan premeditated and clever. In my view it would be foolish to involve oneself in a murder plot not knowing all the accomplices to the murder. This is one of the reasons why I believe this murder plot was not only unthinkable but unworkable from the UDR Four point of view.

Allen was arrested on Monday 3 December 1983 and taken directly to Castlereagh. There he was read extracts from alleged confessions of Latimer and Bell, which he said were unbelievable. Allen in a *Voir Dire* dated 20 and 21 May 1986 gave evidence concerning the circumstances that he claims forced him to make a confession to a murder he did not commit. In it he claims he was put under pressure and 'I felt I was going to have to compromise some way ... about the situation.'[25] He further claims that the interrogating officers were forceful and each time he protested his innocence he was roared at and called a liar by the interviewing officers. He claims he was brought to a point where he believed Latimer and Bell had done something wrong and he should try to distance himself from that. If he did not, he believed, the consequences for him would be far worse. Allen was accused of making a series of verbal confessions which were later put into statement form. He challenged their admissibility on the grounds that they were induced by ill-treatment. In the *Voir Dire* Allen said that the interviewing became aggressive, at one point he claims that Detective Constable Robert Peacock smacked him on the side of the face.[26] This Allen recounted made him break down and cry claiming that he was terrified and frightened of what could happen next.[27] Allen hoped that by agreeing with what the detectives put to him they would, to use his expression, 'take them off my back for a while'.[28] Allen denied making a statement but claimed that it came from the recorded question and answer session.

In his judgment Lord Justice Kelly said:

> The detectives denied anything improper had occurred. He was not struck at all. It was true that he broke down and cried and was taken outside into the corridor. They found it difficult to say what caused him to break down. In the opinion of one (Detective Constable [William] Martin) it was because it was revealed to him that Latimer had been identified dressed in a tartan cap and blue anorak but it may have been that he saw he was being 'related to the crime' and that he was in a strange place being interviewed as a murder suspect by tems *(sic)* of detectives. He was taken outside to compose himself.
>
> It was put to the detectives that they realised that he was 'a softie' and 'got stuck into him verbally', that Detective Constable [William] Martin 'roared' at him and shouted at him and this caused his break down. Detective Constable [William] Martin admitted that he shouted at him from time to time.[29]

Lord Justice Kelly then gave his reasons for believing the detectives' claims and for disbelieving Allen's claim that he had been mistreated or struck in the manner he alleged until he broke down. In his judgment he said:

> ... I believe in the case of Allen his break down was much more likely to have been brought about by the situation he found himself in, being questioned as a murder suspect in Castlereagh and emotionally precipitated by the evidence implicating him ... I have no difficulty in dismissing Allen's assertion that he was physically assaulted.[30]

The judge accepted that Allen must have felt under pressure due to the nature of the circumstances he found himself to be in. However, that pressure was by no means 'oppressive to the degree that it "so affects the mind of the subject that his will crumbles and he speaks when otherwise he would have stayed silent" to use Lord MacDermott's often quoted words'.[31]

Lord Justice Kelly went on to state concerning Allen's confession:

> Nevertheless I believe the recorded questions and answers were used at interview 9 much more extensively to direct the order and content of the written statement han (sic) Detective Constable [Henry Kenneth] Nixon and Detective Constable [John] McAteer are prepared to admit. They were not in this as forthcoming as a court expects. But it does not follow that all of their evidence is lies although naturally one looks closely at the rest of it.[32]

Lord Justice Kelly was satisfied beyond all reasonable doubt that Allen's confession be given full weight.

The four men do not accept the verdict. Their case is they were trapped in an emotional labyrinth; that they were easy prey for the detectives who used their professional skills developed from dealing with hardened terrorists to induce confessions. Each side found itself in a precarious situation. On one side were detectives used to dealing with the interrogation of terrorist suspects who are in a diametrically opposite corner. On the other side were regiment members who upheld the law and were instruments of the law. They were brought up to respect the rule of law and joined a regiment dedicated to the protection of the community and maintenance of law and order. They say they broke under the pressure, hoping that the very absurdity of their confessions would expose it all as hideous nonsense.

This face-to-face confrontation between two sides of the same law placed Neil, Noel, James and Winston in jeopardy. Their hope that the police were their friends and that this relationship would be their salvation not their downfall, was the double jeopardy. Lord Justice Kelly proved the point when he cited that their position as soldiers meant they were hard enough and astute enough to withstand pressure and would not succumb to physical or mental pressure without lodging the strongest possible protest.[33]

A more personal view of the four accused and the nine others implicated makes Lord Justice Kelly's statement and judgment unsatisfactory. Others have expressed disagreement with his judgment – for example Rev Hamilton Skillen, the past president of the Methodist Church who has maintained contact with the four men, claims he is convinced of their innocence based upon his many years of experience in judging human character.[34]

A former Moderator of the Presbyterian Church, Dr James Mathews, claimed it was 'very disturbing, not because they belonged to the UDR but for the sake of justice'.[35] In relation to the Guildford Four Case Ludovic Kennedy summarising his experiences on human character has said: 'It has been my experience, in more than thirty years of studying miscarriages of criminal justice, that guilty people asserting innocence (which contrary to popular belief, few do) express themselves differently from innocent people asserting innocence'.[36]

I am convinced that the four men of the UDR Four Case clearly fall into the category of expressing themselves 'differently'. In my view one of these different qualities would be the fact that for over seven years they have unswervingly denied guilt in a convincing manner. Those who maintain their innocence over such a long period against all the odds, as these men are doing, are in the majority of cases, I feel, telling the truth.

3

THE TRIAL

'Armagh plea for calm', was a headline in the *Irish News* one month after the murder of Adrian Carroll.[1] Northern Ireland's political leaders were considering the Prior (Secretary of State, James Prior) initiative of rolling devolution at an assembly-type parliament in the province. Republican terrorists, in a sustained effort to destabilise this process and thus hamper progress, were in the midst of an increased terror campaign. Armagh had been the scene of increasing IRA and INLA terror. In February 1983 Sergeant Gordon Wilson (29) was killed on the eve of his birthday when he detonated a booby trap bomb at the derelict Albert Bar in Lower English Street while on duty. Such violence was not new to this religious capital of Ireland. Armagh's geographic position and the religious and political make up of its people make it easy prey for the sectarian motivations and violence that sweep the province. Armagh is a city of high associations. It is the site of St Patrick's Cathedral, one of the most beautiful cathedrals, containing many architectural masterpieces. Yet this religious capital is also a hot-bed of discontent. The two religious and political faces of Irishmen come together here. In 1969 it was the site of one of the most ferocious civil rights disturbances.

In 1983 Loyalist terrorist groups had embarked upon a tit-for-tat effort to redress the tide of Republican incidents. The plea for calm came the day after Edgar Graham, Official Unionist member of the Northern Ireland Assembly for South Belfast and Constitutional Law Lecturer at Queen's University, had been murdered outside the university. Councillor William Johnston, an Armagh Unionist, in a statement warned the people to 'cool it and realise tit-for-tat killings are leading nowhere.'[2]

The pleas for calm were answered by a bomb blast two days later in Upper Irish Street in Armagh. Two young policemen were taken to hospital after a booby trap bomb exploded. A third officer was badly shocked. Such scenes of horror were not exclusive to Armagh. A sincere fear was expressed by leading churchmen and politicians that if the Chief Constable and the Secretary of State were not able to deal adequately with this 'unacceptable level of violence' then the situation throughout Northern Ireland could deteriorate.[3]

Such fears emerged after a bleak year of exasperation for the security forces – 21 soldiers, 7 members of the UDR and 12 policemen were killed by the IRA and INLA, and 57 civilians also died.[4] A year of inhuman butchery was followed by a series of RUC counter-terrorist 'successes'. Altogether the RUC elite HQMSU attacked and killed 5 IRA and INLA members in incidents called 'shoot to kill'. A sixth person, with no connection to any organisation, Michael Tighe was also killed.[5] An enquiry and investigation initiated by Sir Barry Shaw, then DPP, into the alleged cover-ups by RUC on how these terrorists were confronted and shot, brought Assistant Chief Constable John Stalker of the Greater Manchester Police to Northern Ireland in an investigation for the truth.

Autumn 1982 to Autumn 1983 was the year the IRA embarked upon a double platform strategy of the ballot box in one hand and the armalite in the other.[6] As a response to, and aftermath of, the hunger-strikes the IRA re-organised both politically and to a degree militarily outside the prison. Instead of orders coming from within Long Kesh the IRA were now more prepared to adapt themselves to the 'flamboyant' and one-off terrorist attacks in an effort to prove they had not 'gone soft', because of their emerging political wing – Sinn Féin.

In October 1982 Sinn Féin took 10% of first preference votes in the Northern Ireland Assembly elections. Tactically to avert a split the IRA had then to reassure its hard-liners that they had not gone soft. The campaign from Autumn 1982 to December 1983 left them in no doubt. That year notched up on the IRA/INLA roll of dishonour horrific acts of slaughter such as the Droppin Well pub bombing, Ballykelly, and the Darkley killings. Locally recruited RUC and UDR men became IRA/INLA 'daily bread' victims.

Since 1976, government policy on Northern Ireland has been to hand over the role of security to the local police, RUC and the UDR, thus taking away the need for the British army, and in effect relieving the politically unwanted vision of soldiers' coffins returning to England. In practical terms this meant the IRA/INLA campaigns had to be paid in 'Protestant' blood. This enemy was more vulnerable, as off-duty UDR and RUC men are considered soft targets for the IRA. The IRA tactic then was to hit them as hard and as often as possible in order to sicken and weaken resolve, and deter others from joining. That, the terrorists hoped, would leave Ulster defenceless and achieve a British withdrawal.

The brutal reality was a series of UDR and RUC corpses including several civilian 'mistakes'. The IRA's cavalier attacks had overstepped all boundaries of what the police and army were used to. The temperature in Northern Ireland was being raised. Fears that the security forces would retaliate out of hand were voiced. Some even expressed fears that Northern Ireland was helplessly being pushed toward civil war. There were fears that a Loyalist backlash would ensue if security measures were not stepped up in order to stem the violence. Some even feared that members of the security forces would take the law into their own hands in retaliation for colleagues' deaths.

On 9 December 1983 a number of UDR men were charged

with the murder of Adrian Carroll. The Loyalist community was shocked by such charges brought against members of the regiment. Nationalist opinion was the reverse. Since its inception the Ulster Defence Regiment has been maligned as a Protestant bigoted force. This attitude persists to the present day – as recently as 20 February 1990 in a BBC Panorama documentary it was charged with being a 'Protestant militia'.[7] Such labelling over the last 20 years has discredited and besmirched the name of the whole regiment among people who believe the 'bad' and 'seedy' rather than accept the facts. Allegations that the Ulster Defence Regiment is predominantly Protestant are misleading when one looks at the real reason why there are so few Roman Catholics in its ranks. Roman Catholic members of the UDR were attacked and killed by the IRA in a successful effort to hinder them from joining. In the first five years after the UDR was established the IRA were killing two Roman Catholic members to every one Protestant member. Little wonder a depletion in Roman Catholic members occurred. Charges that Roman Catholics left because of harassment from Protestant colleagues are unfounded.

The Ulster Defence Regiment was primarily established to assist the RUC and British army in fighting the terrorism of the IRA. From 1981 to 1988 there have been 3,739 Republican terrorist incidents compared with 278 Loyalist incidents. It is under such pressure that the security forces keep their heads, and demonstrate a professional demeanour and discipline.[8]

Despite the incriminatory picture painted by some Nationalists of the UDR, John Hume in a speech to his party conference in November 1988 revealed that the UDR were responsible for only 0.28% of deaths in Northern Ireland, Republicans have killed 250 times as many human beings as the UDR.[9] Attitudes reflecting the idea that the UDR are now part of the problem and not an attempt to solve it, place the regiment in a precarious position of being under constant fire from critics.

Neil Latimer was in police custody on 5 December 1983. That day Séamus Mallon, deputy leader of the SDLP, echoed the Nationalist viewpoint before a single charge was brought, that the UDR should be disbanded and that the first step, 'should be to stand down the regiment in Armagh'. Altogether ten UDR soldiers from Armagh were being questioned by the RUC concerning the Carroll murder. Of them five soldiers were charged with his murder, a sixth McMullan, was charged with failing to give information likely to assist in their apprehension. Because of the evidence only four were convicted, despite some doubts over the corroboration of the confessions the four men signed. The other soldier not convicted, Colin Worton, had his case discharged as the judge would not rule his confession admissible as evidence. The crown acknowledged there was no other evidence against him. Séamus Mallon encouraged this lack of confidence in the regiment with a statement that there could 'be no solution to the political problems in the North while the UDR remained in existence. If peace and stability are ever to be created then this body can have no role to play'.[10]

With these arrests the political vampires appeared to have their pound of flesh despite rallying calls of support for the UDR throughout the province's council chambers. It was under these political circumstances that the UDR Four were charged – was there a pre-trial by the press and politicians? Were the UDR Four guilty before they had a chance to prove their innocence? Obviously the fairness of such comments must be called into question. The four men now in prison feel that they were fall guys in a wider conspiracy to alienate the whole regiment at a time when the cards were most heavily stacked against them. The question begging to be asked – could a fair trial take place under these circumstances? Some legal experts have said that if a jury trial had been in operation the UDR Four case would never have gone to court. There is no evidence or suggestion that Lord Justice Kelly was prejudiced by the pre-trial publicity. However, justice must not only be done but must be seen to be done.

The UDR were not the sole element of the Northern Ireland security system feeling the public wrath of their critics. The RUC were themselves under attack and its Chief Constable, Sir John Hermon, was doing his utmost to ensure that the RUC was seen as professional and committed to impartial law enforcement.[11] Counterblasts against the RUC were increasing due to an ongoing criticism that their members were operating in clandestine units and pursuing an unofficial policy with official backing of 'shoot to kill'. This accusation had been made a year before Adrian Carroll was murdered when his brother Roddy Carroll, along with one other INLA terrorist, was shot by the police in what became known as questionable circumstances.

The shooting of Séamus Grew and Roddy Carroll on 12 December 1982 was the last of three incidents that shook the RUC from top to bottom. The police system of counter-terrorism was to be placed on the line, their informant – the mole – whose identity was threatened by the Stalker Enquiry, had to be protected. The then Chief Constable, Sir John Hermon, along with other senior ranking officers, made a concerted drive to prove the professionalism of the police.

It was incidents like this one and the shooting of Eugene Toman, Seán Burns and Gervaise McKerr on the Tullygally Road; the shooting of Michael Tighe and Martin McCauley near Lurgan; and the Grew/Carroll incident, where the RUC were obtaining results by a means which many believed to be outside the rule of law, that, in 1984, brought John Stalker the Assistant Chief Constable of the Greater Manchester police to Northern Ireland for what became known as the Stalker Enquiry. The security forces were under suspicion. Had the RUC not questioned and charged the UDR Four the Nationalist community would have called it a white-wash. There was enormous pressure on the police to get results.

At a meeting held on 31 July 1990 when Máiréad Maguire, formerly Máiréad Corrigan of the Peace People movement, asked Norman Bell the father of Noel Bell, to come along with her to meet Fr Denis Faul, it was disclosed that Fr Faul had, having met a woman, who became Witness A, made it his business to meet senior RUC officers, 'Chief Constable and higher', requesting that a patrol of UDR soldiers be arrested and questioned by the RUC.[12] The request was made before 29 November 1983 when Latimer was arrested. Demands for UDR arrests from sources outside the RUC were evident immediately after the Carroll shooting. This point has been emphasised by the meeting the Bells had with Máiréad Maguire and Fr Faul. Fr Faul has described this accusation as fiction. In an article in the *Sunday Independent*, by John Devine, on 17 February 1991 he denies all allegations made by Nobel prize-winner Máiréad Maguire and Margaret and Norman Bell. He also rejects the idea that he spoke to Sir John Hermon. He said:

I never met Sir John Hermon, or any government minister in connection with those matters.

In the same article Sir John confirmed this and said:

With regard to the apparent suggestion in the documents submitted to the Secretary of State that I met Fr Faul in relation to the so-called 'Armagh Four', I state categorically that there is no substance or truth in that statement.
I have never had any such meeting with any of these people, or with any other people concerning this matter.[13]

It is essential to grasp the crown's case against the UDR

Four. In my view there lie the seeds of its own downfall. The prosecution scenario is not only based upon a ludicrous and absurd theory but lacks in credibility and evidence from start to finish.

The day following Carroll's murder the *Belfast Telegraph* issued a public appeal for help on behalf of the RUC. It was clear that the police had a certain set of leads to follow.

Firstly, the Protestant Action Force who claimed the murder of Carroll had also claimed the murder of Sinn Féin election agent Peter Corrigan in Armagh the year before. In their appeal the police said the PAF was a 'label of convenience' for a Loyalist killer gang. 'An intensive hunt was being mounted to track down the murderer.'[14]

Secondly, a clear description of the murderer had been issued. This information was gleaned from Elaine Faulkner – the only eye-witness to the murder. Elaine Faulkner who worked in Dawson Street, just above Abbey Street where Carroll was murdered, was posting letters at Abbey Street post office. As she made the return journey up Abbey Street her attention was caught by a man who walked past her. She recounts in a statement that she got as far as the back of the post office when:

> I saw this same man reach into his duffle coat and pull out a gun with a long barrel. This man then ran into the laneway to his left where there are some houses. I then heard 2 shots.[15]

Elaine Faulkner made a positive identification of the gunman. She went to the police station and gave details of what she saw. From her description a photo fit was drawn up. Her statement continues:

> I froze and I then ran past the entry on the other side of the road and I saw a man lying up the entry a short distance ... I got scared.[16]

She ran back to her place of work and got her employer to take her to the police station. Her description of the gunman was lucid:

> 20-25 years, about 5' 1" or 5' 2", small build, wearing a light blue duffle coat and a tartan or check cap, small sort of face and he had a light moustache and wore ordinary type glasses with a gold rim. I would know this man if I saw him again. I think he had dirty fair hair, tidy cut, and had on light casual shoes, that's all I seen.[17]

Miss Faulkner was to be a crown witness. After all it was her identification of what the prosecution labelled the 'disguise' that was required to corroborate what another witness, Witness A, saw.

As it turns out Elaine Faulkner is a most accurate witness for the defence because she was adamant the person she had seen was not Neil Latimer. Elaine Faulkner knew Neil Latimer to speak to as he lived close to her. If she was able and honest enough to give the police so much information, would she then lie about his identity? Would Neil Latimer, if he was the murderer, have, on recognising a neighbour, continued to carry out a murder in front of her? The prosecution asked the court to believe part of Elaine Faulkner's testimony and ignore the rest.

The third lead was a Cortina car that was seen speeding away from the scene of the murder immediately after the shots were fired. The car was later found abandoned a short distance away at Cathedral Close. It formed part of the prosecution investigation in the murder theory not consistent with members of the UDR having committed the murder. The tests carried out on it by the police must surely have required forensic tests. In repeated requests from myself, my father, Peter Robinson, Ken Maginnis and the families, for access to the forensic evidence relating to this car, the police have been less than co-operative.[18] No police file on the Cortina car has been produced by the police for the solicitors to examine. This Cortina car was found on the evening of the murder, and traces of fibres from the occupants' clothes may have been found and could have been matched with the accused's clothes. Items of Latimer's clothing were taken away and forensically tested for gun-powder residue similar to that found in Carroll's body. No link was established in this respect. I suggest that the RUC should have forensically tested the car for the same gun-powder residue. If any was found then it would have removed suspicion away from Latimer and would have eliminated him from any police enquiry. This apparently was never done.

Fourthly, the RUC had the ballistic evidence from the traces of bullets found in Adrian Carroll's body. These bullets were identified as being from a Smith and Wesson .38. According to the authorities no gun has ever been recovered for this murder, neither has the gun been used in any other incident. In a parliamentary question No 85 Rev. Ian Paisley (Antrim North):

> To ask the Secretary of State for Northern Ireland, if the RUC has in its possession a gun the ballistics of which match the weapon used in the murder of Adrian Carroll in Armagh in November 1983.

Mr Cope:

> This is a matter for the Chief Constable, but I understand that police checks on recovered weapons which it is believed could have been used in the murder of Mr Carroll have not revealed a matching weapon.[19]

From this information, pointing to a Belfast UVF operation, the police investigation led them to several arrests, not of UVF suspects but rather of UDR soldiers in Armagh! These arrests began on 29 November, days after the police received a statement from Witness A.

In this statement Witness A, a woman from the out-skirts of Armagh who Fr Denis Faul claimed was an innocent, simple Catholic woman who couldn't tell a lie, implicated Pte Neil Latimer in a bizarre charade. Witness A's evidence will be dealt with in a separate chapter. However, the bare bones of it are that she saw Neil Latimer, whom she knew, being 'mock-arrested' by UDR soldiers, being taken from Lonsdale Street Technical College and being put into the back of a UDR landrover.[20] The prosecution case neglected to direct itself to how the UDR Four carried out the shooting without the knowledge of the other members of the patrol. The implication, in my opinion, is that they all supposedly knew and were there-fore alleged collusionists. Inability to prove this point seems to undermine the original conviction. She said he was wearing a cap, and gold rimmed glasses (similar to Elaine Faulkner's description of the gunman). That is all Witness A claims she saw; some time later she reported this to a priest, Fr Raymond Murray, who is renowned for his attacks on the UDR. Her statement was the starting point from where the prosecution's scenario was made, and from where the police investigation of the UDR began. On analysis this scenario upon which the UDR Four were convicted was by no means clear but rather foolish.

According to the prosecution, on 8 November 1983 a UDR patrol set out on duty with a plan to kill a Repub-lican.[21] This thirteen man patrol, and a fourteenth man at Scotch Street barrier, were implicated in the UDR Four trial. Four of its members were convicted. If the prosecution case is correct, then nine other associates and conspirators are free. Lord Justice Kelly in his judgment called it an 'audacious murder ... premeditated and clever.'[22] The murder he ruled was carried out by the accused using their positions as soldiers for cover. The scenario upon which they were convicted was by no means clever, but rather foolish to a degree of ludicrousness and craziness. The absurdity of the prosecution case is one of the factors that makes this case cry out for re-examination. Some aspects and facets of it are demonstrably inaccurate, and unworthy of consideration.

The prosecution case claims the following happened:

The accused knew Adrian Carroll worked as a painter and that he signed off work at McCrum's Court each afternoon and walked a certain route to his home in Abbey Street. They resolved to shoot him, and 8 November 1983 was to be the day of this premeditated crime. The soldiers were on duty shortly after midday and their detailings gave them the use of army landrovers as is the normal procedure. While their vehicles and the wearing of uniform provided overall cover for the plan and much of its activity, it would not do for one of its members, who was to be the gunman, to be seen in uniform following Carroll from McCrum's Court, through the city to the vicinity of his home, and shooting him. At 1.30 pm the accused, they say, left Drumadd Barracks for search duty in the Moy Road area on the outskirts of Armagh. This first search lasted over two hours. They then moved on to an area close by the first search area but off the main road, for a second rummage search. At this point, phase one of the murder plan was put into operation. They say Private Winston Allen drove Private Neil Latimer along with Sergeant Walter Roleston into the city to the Technical College in Lonsdale Street. They stopped and left off Latimer, in daylight, and in full uniform without a weapon. It was there outside the Tech, behind a portacabin that he pulled his jeans on over his camouflage trousers, and swapped his army sweater and jacket for a navy sweater and duffle coat, or anorak – this point was undecided. His beret was replaced with a cap, and a degree of disguise was affected by wearing gold rimmed glasses. Latimer was left to wait. Meanwhile Private Allen and

Sergeant Roleston returned to the Moy Road search. The second search was rounded up and his colleagues boarded their four vehicles. The landrovers then did u-turns on a narrow laneway and proceeded to drive back into Armagh by the same route they came in. The time was around 4.00 pm. Their destination was Newry Road RUC Station, the usual route which would have taken them through Lonsdale Street.

Phase two of the murder plan, they say, was then begun. Occupants of two of the returning landrovers played an active part. Accordingly Lance Corporal James Hegan along with Private Colin Worton were in one vehicle and Private Winston Allen accompanied by Noel Bell and Private McMullan were in the other. These vehicles stopped in Lonsdale Street. Hegan parked at right angles to the Technical College. Here the purpose was to pick up Latimer in his disguise. The crown alleged that the clever plan, and ultimate downfall was a 'mock-arrest' staged by the UDR patrol in a charade to convince on-lookers that nothing out of the normal was taking place.

Northern Ireland people, despite the turbulent history of this country, and their acceptance of troop movements, are still a curious people. Arrests in town centres are not normal everyday procedure, and in a mixed city they draw a lot of attention.

Back to the crown case. The central figure in this clumsy charade was Latimer. The soldiers jumped from their landrovers and took up cover position. Bell and Worton disembarked, entered the college grounds, found Latimer, and keeping close to either side escorted him back to Hegan's waiting landrover.

Surprisingly this event in daylight, on a busy street, in front of a college with 200 staff and pupils, happened with only one witness – according to the crown – a civilian, Witness A, who knew Latimer well, and was driving in Lonsdale Street when she stopped close by the UDR road block. She wondered if Latimer was getting married and his colleagues were 'doing him up'.[23] The landrover then, according to the prosecution, left Lonsdale Street and drove along the Mall. In the course of this journey Hegan handed Latimer a handgun which was to be the murder weapon. The landrover stopped in Mall West where Latimer disembarked and walked towards Pinkerton's Yard. Allen's landrover drove on to the Newry Road Station while Hegan and Bell circled the Mall and waited for Latimer to complete his mission. Latimer waited for Carroll to clock off work, stalked him as far as Abbey Street and shot him in front of his home. Latimer proceeded to run back down Abbey Street into the city where the shots had been heard, and down College Street where Hegan's landrover was waiting. This 'civilian' then jumped on board and, while the vehicle drove to the Newry Road Station, Latimer changed back into uniform. Hegan arrived just shortly after the other landrovers had returned.

Simultaneously other events followed this murder, which have bearing on the UDR Four trial. On the same afternoon a 17-year-old clerk, Elaine Faulkner, made a statement to the police. She was the only eye-witness who had seen the gunman moments before the shooting. She gave a more than adequate description that led to a photofit, and she remains positive she can identify that man. Elaine Faulkner's evidence was only accepted in part by the crown, namely the description of the gunman's clothes, and even on this point there are uncertainties on the part of the judge about the type of jacket worn. They ignored the man's features and physique and, more importantly, Elaine Faulkner's adamant testimony that the gunman was definitely not Neil Latimer whom she knew.

A second witness was called to give evidence. This woman also knew Neil Latimer. Unlike Elaine Faulkner it took her several days and possibly as long as two weeks (22 November) to make a statement alleging she saw a more-than-strange event taking place outside Armagh Technical College. Unlike Elaine Faulkner she never went to the police, but rather to two priests, not her own priest but Fr Murray and Fr Denis Faul.[24] Witness A made a statement in the presence of these priests who in turn gave to the police a typed version of her accusations some time between 22 – 29 November. Unlike Elaine Faulkner, this woman wanted to conceal her identity and became known as Witness A. Unlike Elaine Faulkner, Witness A had a police record and was proved to have been untruthful concerning a past court appearance.[25] During the Appeal, Judge Lowry clearly stated, 'No doubt many parts of her evidence were quite wrong.'

The extent and content of Witness A's statement will be dealt with later. She is important because her evidence is the only corroboration of parts of the statements made at Castlereagh. Witness A alleged that she saw Latimer disguised as a civilian being 'mock-arrested' at the Armagh Tech by two colleagues shortly before Carroll was murdered.

In response to this statement Latimer was arrested on 29 November 1983 and, according to the crown, made a statement that evening which implicated him in Carroll's murder, and in a subsequent statement on 2 December a more rounded and fuller confession emerged. Latimer, Hegan, Bell and Allen along with two others, Worton and McMullan, all claimed their statements were forced out of them, and challenged their admissibility (on the grounds they were extracted from them by use of inhuman and degrading treatment) in a 68–day trial which began on 3 March 1986 with a judgment delivered on 1 July 1986. Two of the men were acquitted. Worton because his confession was ruled inadmissible and there being no other evidence he was discharged. McMullan, was charged with failing to give information contrary to Section 5 of the Criminal Law Act 1967. Lord Justice Kelly acceded to his application on the ground that his privilege against self-incrimination amounted to reasonable excuse for failing to give inform-ation. Accordingly he was acquitted.[26] The remaining confessions the judge accepted because of the evidence of Witness A and a refusal to believe the police were guilty of any impropriety in the gathering of the evidence and confessions.

The UDR Four appealed their conviction. The Guild-ford Four case, the Birmingham Six and other cases of a miscarriage of justice have demonstrated there is a deep reluctance on behalf of the Appeal Courts to allow an appeal where the evidence and verdict depend upon state-ments made while in police custody. The Court of Appeal upheld their conviction.

Announcing his sentences – the tarnished image of the UDR was forever established by a judicial ruling – Lord Justice Kelly was adamant that the crime went deeper than those before him. He had to accept that if the crown's case was true then other men including the mastermind walked free. This point was emphasised at the Appeal where Lord Lowry stated, concerning the spin off effect Witness A had in coming forward, 'It was her information which led to the members of the patrol being arrested; then persistent but fair questioning led to four of them choosing to make state-ments about their involvement while others chose to remain silent and have not been charged.'

The next evening the editorial in the *Belfast Tele-graph* referred to 'UDR Images'. That same day the IRA murdered 22-year-old Private Robert Hill while he came off duty in Armagh, signalling their continuing campaign to destroy and dishearten the regiment. Those who had sought to discredit and remove the UDR had a field day. Councillor Tommy Carroll, the victim's brother and Sinn Féin councillor in Armagh, accused senior members of the UDR of collusion with the UDR Four.[27] The Carroll family did not believe justice had been fully done. Teresa Carroll described the four as 'puppets' and wanted further convictions of UDR soldiers.[28] Lord Justice Basil Kelly said of some other soldiers, 'I regret to record that the contents of their evidence, the evidence of the army witnesses ... leads me to the firm conclusion that some members of the regiment got together to distort true events ... with the sole purpose of assisting the accused.'[29]

The hypocrisy of the *Irish News* was in full glare. The editorial on 1 July entitled 'innocents behind bars' told of the miscarriage of justice brought to bear on the Guildford Four, yet when asked by the families of the four men to question the conviction of the UDR Four the next day's heading was adamant, the paper would peddle the Nationalist line, 'Carroll's UDR Killers Get Life'. Their editorial, 'Tragedy of Violence', spoke on the 'two faces of the UDR seen in tragic juxtaposition yesterday'. The paper questioned the reliability of the court, not because it accepted the UDR Four pleas of innocence but asked that stiffer 'recommended minimum sentences' be administered to the UDR Four.

The UDR Four have been convicted of a crime they claim they did not and could not commit. Not only are there many reasonable doubts surrounding the original evidence and statements, but several new factors have been brought to light since the trial. In my view it is more than clear that the UDR Four could not and did not murder Carroll, neither had they any knowledge of that crime. I feel a miscarriage of justice has taken place that strikes at the foundations of our society.

4

Reasonable Doubt

British justice and English law demand that a person must be proved guilty and is innocent until proven otherwise. It continues that they must be convicted of a crime fairly and that conviction be beyond all reasonable doubt. No question marks are permitted to hang over a conviction. Although it is not my duty to prove the innocence of Neil Latimer, Noel Bell, James Hegan or Winston Allen, I would only be deluding myself if I did not say that it is impossible to avoid touching on that proposition. It remains up to the authorities to put their house in order. If it is a distasteful process it still should not in any way affect their duty and purpose of upholding law and order and administering justice.

The purpose of this chapter is to review the evidence and scenario upon which the UDR Four were convicted, and more importantly to review the gaping holes, abnormalities, and numerous reasonable doubts surrounding that conviction. In my opinion the only conclusion possible is that these convictions are unsafe. This is not a matter of sour grapes over a difference of inferences that the Lord Justice made, but a raging dispute over the extent of dangerous assumptions made and the lack of any substantive circumstantial evidence. Serious doubts, defects and flaws have appeared and keep reappearing and will not go away until this case is retried. These reasonable doubts highlight an unsafe conviction based upon a thesis and evidence gravely lacking in credibility.

Not only is it necessary to re-examine the original

evidence and thesis of conviction, but I am obliged to look at other factors and new evidence that has come to light since the trial. All in all, in my view, this mounting criticism of the convictions points to reasonable doubt beyond question. A retrial as the four have consistently demanded would not only be obliging but necessary for the sake of justice.

If then the prosecution scenario of events surrounding the death of Adrian Carroll is wrong, what then happened in Armagh on 8 November 1983? James Hegan wrote to Dr Ian Paisley on 23 October 1989 highlighting exactly what did happen. Here are the salient extracts from that letter:

Dear Dr Paisley,
... On the 07/11/83 an R.U.C. patrol spotted two suspect terrorists coming across fields outside Armagh, to the North of it. At the request of the R.U.C. in Armagh, the Battalion Ops Officer, a crown witness, stated in court that they wanted this area searched. He stated that he informed the 'Company' of this request no later than 10.00hrs on the 08/11/83. He also stated that our original duty for that day had been a foot patrol in the west of Armagh city. When I came in for work that day after 12.00hrs I was briefed and tasked to search this area along with twelve other soldiers. Not one of us knew what our original duty was before coming into Drumadd Barracks, not to mention the search request, we could have been almost anywhere in South Armagh that day. Yet this is the day the trial judge said we picked to shoot A Carroll, how? We left the camp after 13.00hrs in our four landrovers and went to the search area.
When A. Carroll clocked off work at 16.30hrs, his workmate, a crown witness, stated that there was no one standing about and that no one followed him from his work, as he was 25 yds behind him, that there was no one between him and A. Carroll, as he went through the middle of Armagh in broad daylight to his house of Abbey St. (Latimer, the alleged gunman, said in his false statement that he waited for him to clock-off and that he followed him through the middle of Armagh to his house in an entry off Abbey St.)
The girl who saw the gunman in Abbey St, a crown witness, said that she met him [the gunman] at a distance of about 1 foot as he passed her in the street. That she was walking up Abbey St 10 yds behind him, when she

saw him take a handgun out of his pocket or coat and go into the entry. She stated she 'froze' there, then she heard two shots and that the gunman did not come back past her in the street again. (Latimer, in his false statement, said he ran back down Abbey St, down into College St to the bottom of it to be picked up in a U.D.R. landrover.) She stated the gunman was 5'1" or 5'2", she is 5'4" herself, Latimer is 5'10" and she positively identified Latimer in court as not the gunman.

College St then was one of the busiest in Armagh and no one who was there that day has come forward to state that a man was seen running down these streets. Nor did the R.U.C. constable, a crown witness, who was coming up it slowly ... on patrol ... He stated also that he saw no U.D.R. landrovers sitting about.

A woman who lives in Abbey St ... a crown witness, stated that she heard the shots and children screaming ... she rushed to get out and before she opened her front door she heard a shuffle of feet going up the street ...

It is obvious the gunman went up Abbey St. At the top of it there is a security barrier ... This is where I believe the gunman's car was waiting for him. The archbishop's gardener, a crown witness, stated that he heard the shots and a few minutes later he heard a car travelling fast down Cathedral Close from the direction of Abbey St. He looked over the wall and saw two men in a blue MK 4 Cortina, but he could not I.D. them. This car was found that night a short distance away in a car park ... It had been stolen two months before in Belfast.

The search was called off at 16.25hrs and we left the area at 16.30hrs approx, taking a longer route to the R.U.C. Station in Armagh via Lonsdale St. En route, the third and fourth landrovers got separated from the first two due to traffic. The first two stopped in Lonsdale St for a short period until 3 and 4 caught up with them there. On doing so 1 and 2 moved off and 3 & 4 followed them on to the station. I was the front seat passenger in the third landrover with Latimer driving and a Pte Worton in the rear. On reaching the station we were informed that there had been a shooting off Abbey St. I and the other members of the section were then tasked to set up a V.C.P. [Vehicle Check point] on the main Armagh–Portadown road, to check the identity of everyone leaving Armagh. We were also informed who had been shot before leaving the station. While at the V.C.P. I received from the Ops Room a description of the gunman which stated, age early twenties, height 5'1" or 5'2", slim build, clothes a blue duffle coat and wearing glasses ... We finished duty that night after 21.00hrs.[1]

It was after coming off duty that a different story began to come together from questionable sources. The starting point of doubt is clearly the tasking orders issued to the patrol on 8 November. It is universally accepted that when the members of the patrol arrived for duty they were given tasking orders to carry out a search on the Moy Road as indicated in Hegan's letter. It is clear that the UDR patrol would not have known what duty they were on until these tasking orders were received. Yet they were found guilty of a murder with malice aforethought, 'the plan to commit this murder was premeditated and clever'.[2] For it to have been planned they would have required advance notice of their duties that day. If, as it was believed, the patrol were to be on foot patrol and they were then informed that the police requested them to carry out a search on the other side of Armagh then their plans would have been ruined, and would most certainly have been abandoned or at least postponed.

A thirteen-man-strong patrol went to the Moy Road around 13.00hrs on 8 November. That fact is confirmed. At 16.30 Adrian Carroll lay dying in Abbey Street. Only three hours of preparation would have been available to the patrol to conceive and administer this plot. Is it possible that a clever and premeditated murder could have been implemented in that short space of time? Such a scenario requires a stretch of the imagination – the acceptance that a collusion theory on a grandiose scale existed for the purpose of taking of the life of a man who was not even an active terrorist, bluntly a soft target. Over 140 UDR soldiers were on duty that day in the Armagh area. Such collusion would have broken along the chain of command. Only an idiot would have planned a murder under these circumstances and with such odds stacked against him.

What then of the four accused? One man, the alleged

gunman Neil Latimer, regarded by many as a joker by nature, too unsteady to be taken seriously. Another man, Winston Allen only joined this section of the UDR five days before Carroll was murdered. Would an unknown quantity have been brought into a murder plot at such short notice? Allen's personal Christian beliefs would have made even the thought of such an act anathema to him. The third man, a career soldier, Lance Corporal Hegan. Would he jeopardise his wife, family and passion for army life on a fault-riddled plan? The fourth, just out of his teens, was according to evidence at the trial unstable. Would he have been able to perform a role which involved coercing Hegan into handing over the gun for the murder? Why go to the bother of an alleged false arrest in an area where an untold number of witnesses would have been present? The obvious place where the gunman could disguise himself was in the seclusion of the search point. He would have time and peace to remove his uniform and disguise himself before being driven directly to the Mall where he could follow the victim. But no, this was too straightforward. A charade of disguises, a mock-arrest, and an extraordinary inexplicable 'carry-on' was, according to the crown, under way. All in all, an effort to divert attention when in reality such a plan was screaming for the attention and curiosity of any passer-by. The whole point is that this elaborate alleged plan of a mock-arrest was simply unnecessary, yet it is the central feature of the prosecution argument.

The Technical College was chosen as 'the safe place' to effect a degree of disguise. Was this sensible for the alleged UDR gunman to go there and disguise himself? From the early 1980s RUC and UDR personnel were not permitted to use the canteen facilities at the Technical College, a security measure taken for their own safety. Those employed at the college in Lonsdale Street, and the students attending, were of mixed religion. This prohibited area and possible hostile facility was allegedly used as a 'safe haven' where Latimer could disguise himself. This suggestion, in light of the prohibition and the attention that such a stunt would draw, rules this suggestion unworthy of consideration. Not only would common sense overrule the contemplation of this but evidence points and I believe will undoubtedly prove that this charade simply did not happen.

What is more, the headmaster of the college produced a list of almost two hundred cleaning, auxiliary and academic staff and students who had been in the vicinity where Latimer was supposed to have changed. It is alleged that Latimer changed in broad daylight from his army uniform, without any backup. From this diverse crowd of would-be witnesses not even one came forward suggesting that they even saw a soldier. Neither did anyone else, apart from the mysterious Witness A, see the mock-arrest. Latimer is supposed to have changed just below, and in full view of, the headmaster's office window. The lunacy of the idea is compounded further when one hears the suggestions tendered as to how Latimer effected his disguise. It is suggested that he pulled jeans or dark trousers over his camouflage military issue trousers. This would in itself be an extremely difficult operation to carry out. It is further suggested that he removed his disguise while in the back of the landrover, yet the rovers used had no back doors so this too would have been performed for all to see.

Going back to the Moy Road, Walter Roleston, the sergeant of the platoon claims that he remembers well the day in question. He gave orders how the various searches were to be carried out and he remained very much the man-on-the-spot with full control of the search operation. Roleston vividly recalls, 'the day closing in'.[3] The drizzle began to thicken and, 'a haziness came over the search area'.[4] Believing it would be unsafe for the patrol to continue the search he called them back to the landrovers at 16.26hrs, when they began the return journey. The usual procedure of a route in and a separate route out was maintained. The landrovers route out was a longer route than the route to the search area. These times are substantiated by twelve other UDR witnesses along with two civilians who were on the road at the same time and have since come forward with statements. Taking the times as accurate it would have been physically impossible for the landrovers to drive to Lonsdale Street, mock-arrest Latimer, drive to the Mall where Latimer had to make his way to Carroll's workplace, wait for him to clock off, then follow him to Abbey Street, shoot him and return to College Street for his pick-up. All this would have to be carried out in the space of ten minutes. It would have to run like clockwork. This time does not give any consideration for delays such as a build up of traffic on the Armagh approach roads, or the chance that Carroll was not going directly home. None of the soldiers deny being in the landrovers in Lonsdale Street. It was for them *en route* to the Newry Road RUC Station where they were heading. Neither do any of the soldiers deny that the landrovers waited outside the Technical College until they all caught up with each other having been dispersed between the traffic.

The prosecution thesis would suggest that the four landrovers u-turned on the narrow Drumcairn Road in order to pick up Latimer on time. Such clumsy manoeuvres for a liaison would only have gained seconds not the necessary minutes the stunt would have required. The whole idea is inconceivable. A more plausible theory is that the gunman waited somewhere along the approach road toward Abbey Street, saw Carroll and then followed him up Abbey Street to carry out the murder. Timing in this instance would have been less critical and reliant upon the victim.

The crown case is based upon the assumption that one landrover would leave the Moy Road search area with Latimer, Allen and Roleston on board. It would drive to Lonsdale Street, drop Latimer off and return to the search area where it would join the other three landrovers and proceed back to Lonsdale Street to pick up Latimer. On arriving at the Technical College the UDR members would embark upon a charade designed to fool any suspecting onlookers. The landrover, it is alleged, then broke away from the main convoy, drove to the Mall and dropped off Latimer. As Latimer proceeded to McCrum's Court where Carroll was working, the landrover circled the Mall and then reversed up College Street (a one-way street) where it waited for Latimer to return. Meanwhile, Latimer is supposed to have followed Carroll from his place of work (despite a testimony from a workmate that no one followed him) to his home in Abbey Street where he was shot.[5] Latimer then is said to have made his way through the centre of Armagh, through English Street and down College Street where he met the waiting landrover.

This is an elaborate story which is quite fantastic. The whole idea of using the cover of the patrol's normality is lost. The premise that collusion between several UDR officers occurred is without standing and has never been elaborated upon. All this happened in Armagh without a witness. Why no witnesses to such traffic-stopping frolics? Was it that they were so effective that they worked, or could it be that they did not and could not have happened? The mock-arrest in broad daylight, involving the co-operation of several other soldiers with at least two hundred potential witnesses there to see – only one mysterious witness came forward who claimed to see the mock-arrest take place. On the 9 June during the trial this witness said: 'I said I have even thought about retracting my evidence because I don't believe them men were guilty'.[6] Since the trial this witness, Witness A, has in a radio interview with Brendan Wright of RTE, said 'the whole thing is not right, the whole case has never been right from the start'.[7] This surely renders the core of the prosecution case unbelievable and unacceptable. If we follow the prosecution case through there is no apparent logical explanation for several factors. What happened to Latimer's uniform which he left at the Technical College? According to Witness A, Latimer had both his hands in his pockets when being escorted from the college grounds.[8] The other soldiers were seen carrying only their own rifles. Although apparent hole-picking, this is a necessary exercise if the credibility of the prosecution case is to be established.

At the Mall a civilian, dressed in tartan cap, blue duffle coat (or brown anorak?) and wearing glasses, jumped out of the landrover. No one witnessed this. Why after going to the lengths of making a mock-arrest in Lonsdale Street was the cover suddenly blown at the Mall? That same landrover circled the Mall, and then reversed up a one-way street (College Street), which if it happened would surely have been noticed.

A running man, supposedly Latimer, then ran down College Street past an RUC mobile patrol, moments after shots had been fired, and jumped into the back of the waiting landrover. Again no witnesses came forward, neither is any explanation offered for the lack of, say, a second mock-arrest! Any strength the prosecution case could have derived from a UDR plot to kill would have been the emphasis on the normality of the troop's movement that day which would have acted as a blanket for their illegal activities. The prosecution theory goes out of its way to be abnormal.

Half-past four in the afternoon in most towns is the beginning of rush hour when commuters begin to make their journey home. Armagh is no exception to the rule, and would be subject to a build up of traffic on the approach roads and in the main town itself. For the prosecution theory to be true it requires perfect timing. However, the gunman could only go by the timing set by the target. Latimer would have been taking a gigantic risk following Carroll. What if Carroll were to go into Armagh to shop or to have a drink. The plan would be foiled. It is more reasonable, practical and logical for a gunman to be waiting at the corner of Abbey Street and then to follow the victim to his house. If Latimer followed Carroll to his house, why was he not spotted by Carroll's workmate who testified that he saw no one follow Carroll as he walked home? If Latimer was the gunman would he have stopped in his tracks when he saw Elaine Faulkner, whom he knew. It was not Latimer who Faulkner saw that day with the gun. On 11 March 1986, under oath she stated that it was 'definitely not Latimer'.[9]

Probably the most disturbing aspect of the case is the accusation that Latimer then ran down the busy thoroughfare of English Street and then College Street where he is supposed to have jumped into the back of a waiting landrover. It is highly unlikely that a gunman would run into the hands of his captors. Utmost in his mind would be a quiet and safe getaway. The logical way out would be via Dawson Street and Cathedral Close, which lead away from the town centre. There is more supporting evidence and witnesses for this route than the route suggested by the prosecution. A stolen Ford Cortina was found abandoned a short distance away. Two witnesses' testimonies suggest that the gunman ran up Abbey Street to the waiting car where he was driven to another getaway vehicle. I will deal with the alternative case in a later chapter.

The UDR patrol members are adamant that they returned to the Newry Road RUC Station simultaneously. This evidence is corroborated by the testimony of a fourteenth soldier who was in an entirely separate UDR section. Sgt Lowry who was on guard duty at a permanent barrier in Scotch Street, had a clear up-hill view of the entrance to the RUC station.[10] Being a soldier, who better to testify about regiment procedure? He maintains that the landrovers returned simultaneously and not, as the crown suggested, in two groups of three and then later on, one. During the trial the prosecution argued that Sgt Lowry was wrong in his assertion that he was on duty at Scotch Street. The prosecution tendered as evidence a report of duties which showed that this post was manned by RUC personnel on the day of the shooting and not by Lowry and his UDR colleagues. Lowry's testimony was therefore discredited as flimsy and inaccurate. Since the trial new evidence and fresh factors have come to my attention that substantiate Lowry's claim. Firstly, two UDR soldiers who were on duty with him at the time have both made affidavits stating that Lowry's testimony was accurate. Secondly, Lowry's testimony is further corroborated by another point – since the trial a classified military document has been leaked that supports Lowry's testimony that he was on duty at Scotch Street barrier at the time he suggests.[11] I have seen this document and it would be available for the purpose of a retrial. This case must now be re-examined. If this document is substantial proof that the testimony of Lowry is true, the spin-off being that if the landrovers returned together, then the UDR Four could not have carried out the murder of Adrian Carroll. The crown thesis would once again be found wanting.

This startling new factor does not solely rely upon Lowry's word but is corroborated further by a new witness. A high ranking British army officer was working that day in Armagh RUC Station. This man has recently come forward with a statement. Now retired and living in England, he maintains that if the patrol had returned separately, serious questions would have been asked. Because of the serious amount of terrorist activities in the Armagh area the patrols had to stay together for their own safety. They were not permitted to split up and return when it suited them. This new witness was present when the landrovers returned, and he remarked to Roleston on their early return. He was also responsible for issuing fresh tasking orders to them.[12] He too is available to give evidence at any retrial. These facets in this gigantic puzzle show serious doubts about the credibility of the verdict. The UDR Four are confident that when the truth surrounding their conviction is exposed, it will set them free.

Circumstantial evidence was brought to the attention of the court in 1986 and was subsequently played down – the whole episode surrounding the Cortina car, and the testimony of the Archbishop's gardener, James Allen. Mr Allen remembers hearing a Ford Cortina and it seemed to be travelling quite fast away from the direction of Abbey Street moments after he heard the shots that killed Carroll. He looked over the wall and saw the car with two people on board.[13] This aspect of the case remains unexplained. It was ruled peripheral to the case by the trial judge, and at the Appeal was referred to as a 'loose end'. Crucial forensic evidence could well have been uncovered when the car was examined the day after the killing which could be of value in identifying the real gunman. These tests have never been made available to the defence.

Communications with the police on this subject have run up against closed doors. Requests for access to police files relating to the car found abandoned at Market Square have been ignored and turned down. Official requests have also been put on the long finger. The following request was made on 3 May 1990 to Mr W. Monahan:

> Is it possible to see the RUC file on the Cortina car that was used in the murder of Mr Adrian Carroll in Armagh in November 1983. We know that for two weeks the only leads the RUC investigation had was this car and the ballistic evidence from the actual shooting. We feel that a thorough investigation of this evidence could be beneficial to this case.[14]

Mr Monahan replied on 18 May 1990 stating that my comments were noted but that any requests for access to this file would have to come from the prisoner's solicitor.[15] Accordingly, Jim Hegan's solicitor wrote to the police, and six months later this information still remains unavailable.

On the afternoon Carroll was murdered, the police were left with three positive leads: the eye witness account and photo-fit given by Elaine Faulkner, the ballistic traces left in Carroll's body and the Cortina car. The first two weeks of police investigations circled around these pieces of information. The ballistic traces could, prior to the 1983 killing, point to other PAF/UVF incidents in Belfast and Lurgan. The Cortina car pointed to a Belfast connection. This connection must be traced and fully explored. I believe that particles from the gunman's clothes could have been left in the car. The fact that there is no link to this stolen car and the accused is a point that has never been given its due weight or consideration. If we link the testimonies of James Allen, the gardener, to Elaine Faulkner and the resident in Abbey Street who heard someone who could have been the gunman running away, to the material evidence of the stolen car, we have an alternative case worth answering. At its minimum there is reasonable doubt.

What then of the evidence that holds these men in prison? It is based upon uncorroborated statements signed while in police custody and then withdrawn because the men claimed they were made under duress. What about the testimony of Witness A? The emergency provisions set up to protect human rights backfired dramatically to the detriment of this case.

According to Lord Justice Kelly only one theory is acceptable. Only one witness is to be believed while those witnesses who suggest a different interpretation of the events are marked untrustworthy or mistaken. The assumption that UDR soldiers would feel perfectly at home while under interrogation by the RUC is erroneous. The case of the fifth man, Pte Colin Worton, was dropped due to the inadmissibility of his statement and there being no further evidence to maintain a case against him, he was discharged.[16] Colin Worton claimed that he underwent a brainwashing exercise, became confused and began to doubt his own innocence.[17]

Merlyn Rees, the ex Secretary of State, has studied the case and called for an inquiry into the convictions. The men themselves have asked that the Secretary of State, Peter Brooke, recommend that the case be returned to the courts for a retrial. In view of the nagging doubts, flaws and inconsistencies in the original case and the fresh factors that have come to light, along with the new evidence, their claim that they were unfairly and unjustly convicted deserves an answer. The fact that the credibility of the police and the conduct of certain officers has been called into question by other members of Her Majesty's Forces places an imperative upon the government to order an independent enquiry into this case. If the RUC do not accept such an enquiry then perhaps another police force from England could be permitted to carry out that enquiry.

5

Police Evidence

On 24 July 1989 Ian Stewart, the then serving Minister of State for Northern Ireland, was adamant that there would be no investigation or retrial of the case of the UDR Four. He was convinced that the evidence against these men was adequate. In a letter to Peter Robinson MP concerning Witness A's reported retraction of evidence, Mr Stewart made it clear that the convictions would remain because of the confessions:

> As you are aware all the evidence presented at the trial of the soldiers, including the allegation that their confessions were obtained either by physical ill treatment or by other improper methods was very carefully considered by the trial judge and again later by the Court of Appeal. It is also clear from the judgment of the Court of Appeal that even if Witness A's evidence was discredited ... there was sufficient other evidence to secure the convictions.[1]

The other evidence referred to which secures these convictions is the statements made by the men while in police custody in Castlereagh. These statements are corroborated only by Witness A's evidence. The alleged confessions were withdrawn by the four men who claimed they were induced from them while under pressure. It is only fitting that a full examination of this evidence is made. At the trial and *Voir Dire* of Bell, Latimer, Hegan and Allen, these statements were examined for credibility. Lord Justice Basil Kelly accepted them as a true and proper reflection of what occurred in Armagh on 8 November 1983. Yet certain discrepancies were highlighted but the judge did not consider them to be important enough to warrant reasonable doubt.

Uncorroborated evidence is probably the most controversial weapon the prosecutors have in England and Northern Ireland. It is so controversial and divisive that it is not fully accepted in all parts of the UK, such as Scotland. Compounded by the fact that this evidence was upheld by a Diplock court, trial without jury and questionable evidence are indeed ingredients for mistrial and injustice. Various facets of the establishment were alleged to be stacked against the defendants in this trial.

Many would-be sympathisers with the UDR Four are dogged by the assumption, 'Yes, but if I was innocent I wouldn't have signed a statement, I would say nothing, or at least go on asserting my innocence despite the verbal and physical pressure being exerted upon me.' The question that has dogged me most and which deserves careful and adequate consideration is what happened in Castlereagh to Bell, Allen, Hegan and Latimer.

Recalling a visit to Maghaberry Prison to see Latimer, I asked him why did he confess to something he did not do. Obviously tired of being asked that question he replied:

> Unless you've been in Castlereagh you've no idea how you are treated. A Mr Nasty and a Mr Nice Guy. If only some one had given me some idea of what went on, how they could get to you I could have put up some resistance. Like I said before, I just wanted out of the place, if they had given me a gun I would have shot myself – I was so confused.

Latimer made as many as 13 different statements on the murder all offering different angles on the murder. At one point he claimed his brother murdered Carroll. In another statement he said the stolen Cortina car was used.[2] All four men claimed at the trial that certain parts of the statements they made to the police were accepted while the other inconvenient bits were discarded. The trial judge, who it must be said, gave the men's claims careful consideration and rejected them. In retrospect it appears to the

four men that once Witness A came forward the investigation concentrated on obtaining statements from them and
others relative to the scenario as outlined by her. Other
important matters such as the Cortina car now became
peripheral to the investigation and subsequently at the
trial.

In his statement which became exhibit nine, Latimer
claims he shot Carroll twice.[3] He was convicted on this
evidence despite forensic evidence that Carroll was shot
three times.[4] Such erroneous inconsistencies were accepted
by the trial judge. Latimer, the alleged gunman, didn't even
know how many times Carroll was shot, yet he was convicted of his murder. The following statements were made
by Latimer at Castlereagh. They give two conflicting
accounts of the events, and when the following statement
which was made on 29 November 1983 is compared to the
eventual prosecution case, a major turnaround has occurred:

> I want to tell you what happened on the day of Adrian
> Carrolls shooting. The Cortina a greenish/bluish colour
> arrived at my house from Belfast a couple of days before the
> shooting. I don't want to say who brought it down. I put it in
> my father's garage down Bennetts Lane and opened the
> boot and seen the gun. I looked at the gun and she was full of
> rounds. I'm not sure now if the number plates were in the
> boot or I changed them. I put the gun back in the boot and
> closed it down and locked the garage and went up home. On
> the day of the shooting I phoned into work and told them that
> I wouldn't be in to (sic) late and I had to go to the Doctor's. I
> went down to Lonsdale Street that morning in my own car
> and put the duffle coat and cap and the glasses that were in
> the duffle coat in a blue bag under one of the huts. Then I
> went back up home. I messed about up at home and then I
> put my uniform in a white plastic bag and headed off down
> the town to the market, near Pinkerton's where I showed you
> on the map and I got changed into my uniform. I waited for
> the rest of the boys on the patrol to come in for a smoke and
> whenever they came and I had a smoke and headed off with
> them. I walked with them up to the Police Barracks and we
> got into two landrovers. I got my rifle there from one of the

landrovers and said I had to go down to Lonsdale Street. We headed down to Lonsdale Street when it was just getting dark. I went to the back of the hut and got changed into the jeans, duffle coat, cap and shoes. I left my uniform in the blue bag ... I told the rest of the patrol that I had to go somewhere and do something and they said that I just couldn't head off like that. After a wee bit of an argument I headed off and got the car. I went down the top of the Mall and saw that Carroll was still working there painting railings. I drove up round the shambles to Market Street and parked the car there. I left the keys in it on the floor. I headed down to Linenhall Street and waited for a while and then I went into McCrums Court ... and waited there until I seen him. I followed him out of McCrums Court and down English Street. I put the glasses I had on when I started following him. I followed him up passed (sic) the Post Office to where he lived in Abbey Street. He turned round just as he was coming up towards his house and thats where I shot him twice. Then I run off down College Street and into Lonsdale Street. I collected the bags and took the duffle coat off and changed into the denim jacket and then headed off home. I stayed at home until around about 11 o'clock when I took my dog for a walk. I went down around the river where I marked on the map and hid the gun by the side of the river ... I realise that I was wrong in what I done and am very sorry.[5]

The other statement was made three days later, the police then had full access to Witness A's statement which was most likely made on 22 November to Fr Murray and Fr Faul. It was then typed out and at some time between 22 and 29 November Fr Faul showed it to the police who in turn interviewed Witness A. As a result the story Latimer told altered considerably:

I want to tell you the truth about shooting of Adrian Carroll. Me and Jim Hagan (sic) were walking out of the camp after finishing the day before the shooting and Hagan (sic) said to me we're going to shoot Carroll tomorrow and I was going to do the shooting. He said to bring in clothes when you come in to go to work, a jacket and trousers. I just said 'yes'. I came in the next morning and went and got a Rover and brought it over in front of the loading bay. I went up to my car and got my clothes. Then I put the clothes under the seat. I lifted the loose seat and then the lid of a sort of box over the wheel and put the clothes in there and then went into the brief. I came out again and went over to the loading bay and loaded my rifle with everybody else and got into the Rovers. We headed off towards the Moy and Hagan *(sic)* asked me did I bring my clothes and I said yes they're in the back of the Rover. Worton and Bell were in the back of the Rover and they knew what was happening because we discussed it earlier. Then on the way out Hagan *(sic)* told me that Sergeant Rolson *(sic)* would be leaving the search early and I would be going with them. He said I would be dropped off at Lonsdale Street where I was to change behind the Technical School Huts.

We went on out to the search and during the search four of us or five got together at one stage and worked out what was happening. There was me and Hagan *(sic)*, Worton and Bell and I don't know if Sergeant Rolson *(sic)* was there or not. Then just before the search was finishing I headed off with Sergeant Rolson *(sic)* in his Rover. I was in the back and Rolson *(sic)* was in the front I think Winston Allan *(sic)* was driving ... We headed off to Lonsdale Street and I got out just beside the huts in Lonsdale Street and went in behind them and took my clothes with me. Sergeant Rolson *(sic)* headed off in the Rover to the Police Barracks. I put my jeans on over my UDR trousers and I took my UDR jumper and jacket and beret off and put on the other jumper and the duffle coat. Then I waited for the Rovers to come. The Rovers came along I heard them coming and I started to walk out. I put the cap and glasses on and I met Worton and Bell. I got into the back of the Rover and Hagan *(sic)* was driving. We headed off towards the Mall and Hagan *(sic)* handed me the gun over from the front into the back. We got up as far as McCrums Court and we stopped and I got out. I headed up to McCrums Court through Pinkertan's Yard where I waited for Carroll to come to check off. I waited for all the rest of the boys to move off and then I followed him down English Street and up round by the Post Office round by Abbey Lane. He was heading up towards his house and then he turned round and thats when I shot him twice. Then I run off down College Hill where I had arranged to meet the Rover. I got into the Rover at the bottom of College Hill and we headed off up the Mall again and I got changed back into uniform again and then we headed off up to the Police Station. I gave the gun back to

> Hagan (*sic*) and he asked me Did I do it and I said Yes and
> one of the other boys in the back said did anyobody see you
> and I said I don't know I don't think so and then we headed
> on up into the Police Station and just acted as if nothing had
> happened.[6]

At his trial Latimer claimed he fabricated this statement.
The detectives returned to him on the basis of Witness A's
statement and questioned him further. They put it to him
that he played a significantly different part in the murder
– the role he is alleged to have played in the mock-arrest.
Side by side these statements were a contortionist's delight. They differ in every manner possible with the
exception of the number of shots fired.

Latimer's statement does not align itself with any of
the circumstantial evidence. If for instance each point is
taken separately, as Latimer's solicitor has done, one finds
grave disparity. Certainly many questions remain unanswered concerning his conviction. Latimer's solicitor
pointed out the controversial points.

Elaine Faulkner was posting a letter for her employers
in Abbey Street. She came face to face with the gunman,
who, a few seconds later, was to shoot Adrian Carroll. The
gunman was wearing a tartan cap and gold spectacles. He
produced a gun from his duffle coat, so naturally her attention was riveted on him. She was right beside him. The
gunman was about 5'2". He was a very small man. He was
smaller than Miss Faulkner who is only 5'4". Miss Faulkner
went straight to the police and told them what she had
seen. At the trial she was able to tell the judge that the
gunman was not Neil Latimer. She knew Latimer well and
had often spoken to him. Latimer is a tall man about 5'10";
the gunman was a very small man. It was never suggested
that she was lying to the court. She gave her evidence in a
frank and forthright way. Unlike Witness A she had gone
straight to the police and told them what she had seen.
Unlike Witness A there were no inconsistencies or difficult-

ies in her evidence.

At the time the shots were heard a gardener was working in the Cathedral gardens some short distance away from where Adrian Carroll was killed. The gardener heard a car drive past the gardens. He looked over the wall and saw it was a Cortina with two people in it. Later, a Cortina car was found abandoned not far from the scene. There was at least a suspicion that the car had been involved in the murder of Carroll, yet this episode has never been satisfactorily explained and does not fit in with the crown case.

Shortly before the shooting, Witness A claimed she was driving down Lonsdale Street with her son. At the school she saw Latimer wearing a tartan cap and glasses. It looked to her as if he was being mock-arrested by two other soldiers. She heard the news that night and realised that the description of the gunman matched the clothes that Latimer was wearing. However, she did not go to the police for approximately two weeks and only did this having spoken to Fr Faul and Fr Murray. The number of inconsistencies in her evidence which were exposed in the course of the trial arouse considerable doubt as to whether she was a truthful witness. Subsequent to the trial, she has been very critical of the way the police conducted the enquiry. Her evidence gave powerful support to the confessions.

According to an interview in July 1990 between Máiréad Corrigan Maguire, Fr Denis Faul and Mr and Mrs Norman Bell, Denis Faul made his role in the events quite clear. He claimed that a woman came to himself and another priest Fr Raymond Murray with an allegation that she witnessed a strange and peculiar incident. This woman was to become Witness A, the peculiar incident – an alleged mock-arrest. At that meeting Fr Faul claimed that he took this story to a police superintendent in Armagh claiming that a UDR patrol had a large part to play in the murder of Adrian Carroll. He demanded that arrests were made and questions asked. Fr Faul, felt that his accusations would fall on deaf ears, then took his complaint to the top, 'the Chief Constable and higher'. One can only guess that the 'higher', which Fr Faul refused to disclose to them, were NIO officials. At that time James Prior was Secretary of State. The political situation was at boiling point, and there was unrest on the streets for Sir John Hermon, the then Chief Constable, to contend with. (In an article by John Devine in the *Sunday Independent*, 17 February 1991, Fr Faul and Sir John Hermon have denied and rejected all of these allegations – see page 48). It is this allegation of Witness A that is central to the trial and conviction of these men as Lord Justice Kelly said: 'The evidence of Mrs A is of the greatest importance in the Crown case against Latimer'.[7] Fr Faul has since the trial stated, 'Everything she did was honourable, and she acted as urgently as she could, and everything the priests did in connection with the statement was honourable and above board ... I have been taking statements ... for more than 20 years and I would back my judgment as to when a witness is telling the truth. Witness A convinced me as a truthful, decent and responsible person.'[8]

Latimer was interviewed by the police in Castlereagh Holding Centre over a number of days. He had more than thirteen interviews. The police account involves him giving a large number of different versions, when allegedly confessing to his involvement in the murder. In a series of different interviews he gave a series of different versions. In one particular interview he apparently went to the lengths of telling the police that his own brother was, in fact, the gunman. The crown case was that the final version of events, which he gave near the end of his interrogation, was, in fact, the true version. Latimer's case was that the police were pressuring him. The police then put points to him that he agreed with until they had enough to make a statement. Latimer and the others claim they developed a dependency upon the police interrogators. The police insist that this is not a trait normally shown by terrorists who go into such circumstances with a resolve to say nothing. Those charged contested the admissibility of these confessions under the Northern Ireland Emergency Provisions Act, claiming they were subjected to inordinate pressure and improprieties by the detectives at Castlereagh.

During cross-examination Latimer told the court that he became scared. He believed himself to be a quiet man, his sole motive in joining the security forces was to get off the dole, he did not see himself as a fighter. During the trial he said that after his first interview with Det. Con. Henry Kenneth Nixon and Det. Con. John McAteer he felt like a 'Zombie'. 'I was going up the walls,' he said, 'I wanted out of Castlereagh when I was in there, and I came to a stage when I just started going along with whatever they put to me.'[9] Latimer claimed he was shown a list of names of people who were all victims of terrorist killings in the Armagh area. Adrian Carroll's name was on this list. Latimer recalls how the detectives pointed to Carroll's name and said, 'That one's yours, you shot him'. When he denied he had anything to do with it Latimer said a detective started 'shouting and balling' at him.[10]

Latimer could hardly recall his duties and maintained he was on foot patrol until later he was given access to material showing he was on search duty on the outskirts of Armagh. Latimer claimed he

> was starting to get scared ... putting something to me I knew nothing about. They said at ... that interview that I was going down – I was going to get a long jail sentence if I didn't make a statement saying that I shot him. And they said that if I did make a statement I would get out of Castlereagh and I would get bail.[11]

He claims he became a desperate and petrified young man and simply wanted out of this nightmare situation in which he found himself.

The detectives, Latimer claims, accused him of responsibility for the Darkley murders, 'They said I shot Adrian Carroll and Darkley was in retaliation for Adrian Carroll'.[12]

Latimer claimed that the detectives then told him why he was arrested and taken to Castlereagh, 'The man I thought to be [John] McAteer, he says to me that if I was taken to Gough Barracks I would be released in no time at all. I would get out in no time and would not be charged but they have me now and I am in Castlereagh. It is a different story.'[13] At the trial the detectives, who were accused of indiscretion in the gathering of the evidence against the four men, denied all improprieties and the judge found in their favour.

By the time Latimer was shown Witness A's statement he was 'petrified', 'I wanted out of Castlereagh and I wanted them to shut their mouths'. (He felt depressed and was scared.) Two other detectives then interviewed Latimer and he made a statement to them. That was Exhibit 7 which turned out not to be consistent with the crown case. Latimer maintains he told the police what he thought they wanted to hear, in order to get them off his back until he got out of Castlereagh. On leaving Castlereagh, Latimer denied the contents of all his statements as being in any way true.

Latimer says the pressure upon him was intense. Between 29 November and 2 December he was interrogated 19 times. Latimer began telling lie after lie to appease the pressure being applied to him. The bizarre and astonishing web of lies that he told could not be given credibility in any sense. His hope, like the others, was that their absurdity would expose the whole affair as nonsense. Lord Justice Basil Kelly accepted the fact that Latimer told lies to the detectives but said, 'I did not think he was good meaning successful at telling lies in court'.[14] The total unreality of the events was believed by the judge because, in Lord Justice Basil Kelly's words, Latimer 'was in full control of his situation in Castlereagh'.[15] To accept such a statement as credible when one realises how young in age, adolescent in mentality and scared in mind Latimer was, was in my view, wrong. It was because of the complete change in personal circumstances that Latimer and the others confessed. Their personal situation was altered from being soldiers one day to suspects the next, and was devastatingly confusing. Lord Justice Kelly outlined to the court in his judgment that the turning point in Latimer's confession was when he realised he was caught out by Witness A. His role in the mock-arrest had been spotted, yet during the trial this witness had said she had thought about retracting her evidence.

After the trial she said: 'I think they [the police] have tricked me'.[16] She said she had only agreed to make a statement after the police had assured her that they already had 'another witness that was on the scene and made a statement ...' The question is how credible was her statement? Comparing Witness A's statement with that of Elaine Faulkner, who actually saw the killer and said it was definitely not Latimer, throws the the whole case wide open and makes the evidence highly questionable.

The other three men convicted, Bell, Hegan and Allen, have even stronger cases as none of their statements are in any way corroborated. Unlike Latimer who had Witness A's statement against him the police evidence against the other three men consists of alleged confessions, which it could be argued, corroborate each other. However, when one considers the implausibility upon which they are based, that argument is diluted even further. Bell's charge was aiding and abetting murder. His role was that of taking part in an alleged mock-arrest. The crown relies on Bell's confession at Castlereagh to prove all this, and Bell challenged its admissibility on the grounds that it was induced by inhuman or degrading ill-treatment. Bell too alleged he was subjected to immense mental pressure and in one day was interrogated six times while recovering from a hangover. It emerged, during the trial, that Bell lost seven pounds in weight in less than six days, beginning from the time he was arrested

In his *Voir Dire* he claimed that at interview six between 10 pm and 11pm the detectives brought in Chief Supt James Mitchell who 'told me that he had heard a lot about me and that he was leaving at 11 o'clock and that if I told him the truth then he would get me home either that night or the next morning'.[17] But Bell maintained his innocence and the chief superintendent left. This is what Bell claims happened next:

> At eleven o'clock he showed me his watch and pointed it out and said, 'look it is eleven o'clock. I am away now ...' He told me I was stupid and then he left the room ... Detective Sergeant [Thomas] Clements then said, 'Now you are going to tell us' ... He got up and told me to stand up and then he took the chairs that were in the room and he stacked them in one of the corners ... at one stage I said to them,'what do yous want to hear?' and they said 'Only the truth'. I told him then that I was telling the truth and I was not so sure what happened or of the next incident but Detective Constable [John] Shields *(sic)* punched me around the chest area or Detective Sergeant [Thomas] Clements slapped me around the face ... They just kept on shouting at me 'Tell the truth. Tell the truth' ... I told them that I was telling the truth and that no one would believe me ... Detective Sergeant [Thomas] Clements punched me in the testicles ... and I fell back against the wall ... It scared the life out of me ... and I shouted 'What do yous want to hear?' ... I told him I had been telling the truth again and he called me a lying cunt again ... he punched me a second time on the testicles and I fell on to the ground ... I got up and I stood with my hands covering my testicles ... and he told me to tell the truth and I told him that I was telling the truth and he punched me a third time ... He told me first of all to take my hands away. 'Take your hands away. How can I hit you if you are holding your hands like that?' and I tookmy *(sic)* hands away and he punched me a third time in the testicles ... When I was getting up I shouted

'All right, all right I will tell yous'.[18]

All allegations of impropriety were denied by the police. The trial judge accepted that the police were telling the truth and that Bell's allegations were false.

Bell admitted that he was scared of Thomas Clements since his first interview with him. He had believed he was at Castlereagh to help the police with their enquiries, he did not realise that the police believed he had played a part in the murder.[19]

The procedure in custody is that suspects are interviewed and their answers noted. Where relevant they may be presented at any subsequent trial. In the case of three of the men these notes played a critical role in their trial. The police maintained the notes were verbatim records of the interviews in question. This was not accepted by the trial judge. However, he still saw fit to rely on the notes as cogent evidence which is in marked contrast to the weight which Lord Lane thought should be given when such evidence in the Guildford Four appeal case was considered.

The circumstances in that case were different to that of the UDR Four case. There, the Avon and Somerset police in the course of an inquiry into the Surrey police force's investigation of the Guildford bombings discovered a typed document which purported to be an interview with Paddy Armstrong, one of the convicted Guildford Four.

At their trial the police had produced hand-written notes which they said were verbatim contemporaneous records of the interviews with the accused. The discovery and existence of a typed record of the interview undermined the police account that their hand-written notes were in fact contemporaneous records.

There is no evidence, or indeed suggestion, that this occurred in the case of the UDR Four. But Lord Lane took the view that the shadow it cast over the hand-written notes, which were put in evidence as contemporaneous, was sufficient to taint the evidence in its entirety.

His view was that once the police officers had been shown to be lying about the contemporaneous records, then no weight should be given to the evidence contained in the notes. Lord Justice Kelly accepted that the police had not been truthful in their evidence on how the notes were compiled. There was a conflict of evidence among the police themselves. Some said the notes represented a spontaneous account given by the accused during interviews. Another said the suspects had been interrupted at intervals and asked questions to direct them into the relevant areas of the investigation. Lord Justice Kelly took the view that the police evidence indicated that some police officers had lied. However, unlike Lord Lane he did not find it crucial to the case. The lies, he ruled, were immaterial lies which did not go to the heart of the matter.

On 19 October 1989 at the Old Bailey Lord Lane said:

> ... evidence has come to light, thanks to the efforts of the Avon and Somerset police – evidence which shows quite clearly, as is accepted by the Crown, that the so-called contemporaneous records of some of the interviews conducted by the Surrey police officers with Armstrong and relied upon by those officers as they gave evidence were not contemporaneous records at all. What exactly they were may never be known, but it is accepted, and rightly accepted by the Crown, if I may say so, that the manuscript notes produced at the trial were not what the Surrey police officers said on oath they were. The officers, to use Mr Amlot's somewhat anodyne expression, seriously misled the court. In fact they must have lied ...
>
> The first possible explanation is that the typescripts are a fabrication by the police from start to finish, invented by some fertile Constabulary mind: that they were amended to make them more effective and were then written out in manuscript so as to enable the police to produce them as though they were a contemporaneous note of the interrogation. The second possibility is that there was a contemporaneous note; that it was reduced into typewritten form by

someone as a fair copy for some reason or other – perhaps legibility; one does not know – and that it was then amended here and there in order to improve it; and, finally, that it was reconverted into manuscript by the various Surrey officers involved so that it could be produced as a contemporaneous note.

It may be that it was a mixture of those two possibilities, but for the purposes of this appeal it is immaterial which of the two versions is true. In any event the police were not telling the truth about this crucial document in the case against Armstrong. If they were prepared to tell this sort of lie, then the whole of their evidence becomes suspect and, I repeat, on their evidence depended the prosecution case.[20]

Mr McLoughlin, the defence counsel in the UDR case, had the following verbal altercation with the judge, regarding the admissibility of the police evidence:

Mr McLoughlin: ... I'm sure this point has been made many times to Your Lordship. But what I am saying, My Lord, is that where, as here, there are grounds for concern, as I would submit to Your Lordship in due course, that one is looking for clear and cogent evidence about what did happen at a particular interview or a particular stage in the interview. That in order to get any evidence at all about what happened one really goes to the notes. And when one is trying to determine the issue: 'Am I getting cogent and credible evidence', one is really asking: 'Are the notes cogent and credible?' One can't go back from the verbal evidence in court to an earlier statement of evidence, as one might be able to do in certain circumstances, to find out what was said perhaps a month afterwards and test the oral evidence against a more contemporaneous record; what one has to do is go back to the interviewing notes, because the evidence, in fact, consisted of the notes.

It was almost as though we were being asked to accept the interview notes, just handed in to the court as it were, but in this case with the courtesy of having them read to us. And that -- it's difficult, My Lord, to get away from the defects in that kind of evidence. And one is still asked to accept that these notes are in fact almost gospel on the basis that they were contemporaneous records made at the time. And if that

-- if we're put to a position where we have to accept that as being the only evidence that's available, then in my submission one has to look and look with a degree of caution as to just how that claim can stand up. And in my submission when one looks at that claim it can't really stand up. Because what Your Lordship is being asked to believe is that in the course of these interviews, some of them very prolonged, one of them in particular lasting for four and a half hours, being part of a longer interview, that officers were capable of conducting close questioning of a suspect over a wide range of issues and topics and at the same time record a statement of evidence.

Now in my respectful submission, My Lord, that is not a credible proposition. And if the notes are not credible, then in my submission the evidence can't be credible ... These notes, My Lord, and one only needs to look at them --I think Your Lordship does at least have the handwritten notes -- they are written in a form that has not required any editing, they're virtually error free in the sense that nothing that's in them has been corrected, no re-drafting has had to take place. And really, My Lord, one is left to speculate: 'were there other notes that were less complete that were somehow or other used upon which to base these perfectly drafted and edited notes?'

Lord Justice Kelly: I often wish I could take notes as neatly and as carefully as the police in all these cases ... I've heard this point many times, and for some reason or other the police will never admit that there was another copy, something written down quickly at the time and later on transposed into better handwriting and more complete sentences. And of course there would be absolutely nothing wrong with that at all.

Mr McLoughlin: I agree entirely, My Lord. I concede that. But what I respectfully submit, My Lord, is there's a big difficulty for the Crown to get over here when these notes are presented as the definitive evidence about certain issues, because all of those notes have been certified as having been made at the time. And that gives rise, My Lord, to difficulties about them. It may well be that they were written down in a form which wasn't very neat or which wasn't correct and they have been just translated into a more easily read form. One just doesn't know. But my point is, My Lord, irrespective of whatever the implications are in the other context, that if the

Crown evidence in large part is a reading from these notes, then we have to be satisfied that those notes are credible. And they can only be credible if they were made in the way that the police officers say they were made. And if there's a doubt about that issue then there's a dark cloud cast over the notes themselves and therefore the evidence. [21]

These copy book fashion notes are the sole evidence the police had against the remaining three men. They are now subject to electrostatic data testing which will determine whether or not they are an accurate reflection of what took place at Castlereagh. The results of these tests are themselves part of a developing controversy between the police and the solicitors acting for the men. As yet no results have been forthcoming, and any comment upon them is speculation. If the notes are found to be inaccurate and the dicta in Lord Lane's judgment applied then the case against the men must surely collapse. Throughout the trial the validity of the police notes was questioned and at one point the trial judge accepted that the police had lied about the construction of the notes, which is, after all, a crucial factor. Mr McLoughlin continued with his submission to the bench:

The verbal account, My Lord, was either written down as a piece of pure dictation by Bell, as is alleged by Detective Sergeant [Thomas] Clements and Detective Constable [John] Shiels, or it was written down as a result of questions being asked, the answers to which were recorded. Now that's what inspector -- beg your pardon, Superintendent [James] Mitchell had to say. There's, in my submission, a marked conflict of evidence between the three officers, two on the one side and one on the other, about that. That, My Lord, is a crucial piece of evidence.

Lord Justice Kelly: That's another thing in all these cases: the police will always maintain that a verbal account was given in the order in which they'd written it down without interruption most of the time, except an odd question to ask what happened next. Whereas if Sergeant *(sic)* Mitchell goes the length of saying they directed the order of events by questions, if they asked questions to clarify matters and if they asked questions to point the accused to the relevance of what he was saying, they couldn't be criticized.

Mr McLoughlin: Yes. I agree with that, My Lord. The difficulty that that puts the Court in, My Lord, is that one asks why do they not make that clear? And one of the reasons why they might not wish to make it clear is because some misbehaviour did take place and it's an attempt to explain that away.

Lord Justice Kelly: ... They [the police] would never admit that a question at all was asked during the taking down of a verbal or written statement. And in a lot of cases where impropriety was never alleged -- ... and no instructions to allege impropriety were ever given. So it really cuts both ways. It's just a habit or custom of interviewing detectives not to make these admissions because they think in doing so it will detract from its admissibility, whereas it doesn't.

Mr McLoughlin: The difficulty again, My Lord, that the court is placed in is that the implication of that is that the officers tell lies about this.

Lord Justice Kelly: Well, yes, there are lies and lies.

Mr McLoughlin: Well unfortunately, My Lord –

Lord Justice Kelly: Lies which go to the heart of the issue in the case and lies which don't.

Mr McLoughlin: Well, My Lord, the difficulty about that then again is one has to find out whether he's lying about something completely unimportant and not central or are they lying about something which is important and in which they have an interest in denying ...[22]

Here Lord Justice Kelly put his finger upon the whole question, 'there are lies and lies'. It appeared that a set of rules applies to one section of the security forces and another set for another section. Why, for that matter were the police lies accepted as not going to the heart of the matter while the lies of the UDR Four were not given the benefit of the doubt? It seems a ridiculous question – but how else are we expected to interpret those words?

We may, as Robert Kee has observed, compare this attitude to that taken by Lord Lane, the Lord Chief Justice of England, in the Court of Appeal. The point that is now being made is, that if the police were prepared to tell a lie, no matter how insignificant, concerning how their evidence was derived, then that very evidence is contaminated and must be viewed as such. What principle and precedent are we to accept? Have the courts in Northern Ireland difficulty in admitting that the police did wrong?

Continuous efforts have been made to get access to the police notes relating to the UDR Four case so that independent electrostatic data analysis can be made on them in order to determine if they are contemporaneous record, or not. Such tests can determine with a degree of accuracy how the notes were written.

Communications between the various quarters concerned, the solicitors and the police, have taken some time to deliver permission for such tests. However, in a letter dated 31 July 1990, to the solicitors acting for Noel Bell, from the Chief Constable's office, a favourable response has at last occurred:

> The Chief Constable has considered your request for access to original notes, statements and written memoranda.
> He accepts that substantial reasons exist in this particular case for a review of some of the evidence concerning your client (Noel Bell) and has therefore directed that the original interview notes be subjected to Electro Static Detection Apparatus.
> The testing will be undertaken by NIFSL and you will be notified of the results in due course.[23]

The police now recognise that 'substantial reasons exist' for a full examination of the case and this has invigorated, with fresh impetus, the campaign for the men's retrial. The necessity for a full independent enquiry remains.

On the evidence produced to convict Allen and Hegan, gaping holes have emerged. James Hegan was convicted upon an uncorroborated statement in which he allegedly handed the murder weapon over to Latimer. Hegan maintains that this is pure fantasy and that the statement was given under mental pressure. Hegan was a Lance Corporal in

'D' Company. Although he was not considered aggressive he was a firm disciplinarian, who learnt from his sergeant, Roleston, that discipline was essential to good soldiering.

It is alleged by the prosecution and in the statements made to the police that Noel Bell and Neil Latimer bullied James Hegan into giving over the murder weapon.[24] Yet at another point in that same confession he is supposed to have helped plan the murder of Adrian Carroll. Such inconsistencies in its authorship rule it unacceptable and flawed. To believe that James Hegan would allow a younger soldier to bully him with a 'one-liner' into assisting in a cold blooded murder is ludicrous, yet to believe that he allowed himself to be pressurised by older, experienced police officers is believable. Hegan was a servant of the crown used to taking orders from senior men. He claims he was confused by the police treatment and by threats upon his wife and family.[25] He alleges that the police forced his confession on the basis that it would be better for him to agree to their allegations than be 'supergrassed' on by Bell and Latimer.

Hegan was arrested on Saturday 3 December 1983 and taken to Castlereagh Holding Centre. In his *Voir Dire* Hegan gave an account of the interview that followed. He claims that during an interview with Insp. John Brannigan he continually protested his innocence but was shouted down. He was told to stand up, and told he would be hit a 'driver' if he did not confess. Hegan claims a shouting match ensued for thirty minutes until he was struck on both sides of the face by another officer.[26] He too was accused of responsibility for the Darkley massacre. This pressure he claims was sustained for three hours with Hegan standing throughout. When Latimer and Bell's confessions were read to him he became confused and could not understand how they would have been involved. Hegan said he vividly recollected being shouted at in both ears by the detectives accusing him of guilt. He said he was told he would get thirty years and would not be out until 2013. One detective asked if he could swear on the life of his child he was innocent. Hegan said he could. He was then ridiculed and told it was an awful thing to swear.[27] Hegan maintains this type of pressure upset him. He claims his children were threatened with child care and his wife with arrest because his extra kit (additional uniform and army surplus gear kept at his house) constituted stolen goods.[28] When he was confronted with Latimer and Bell he asked them what they were trying to do to him and why they were involving him in this. He says he was then told that Latimer and Bell would turn queen's evidence. Insp. John Brannigan and the other detectives denied all accusations of mistreatment and misconduct. Lord Justice Kelly, in turn, accepted their explanation that Hegan was in fact guilty as charged. Lord Justice Basil Kelly summarised Hegan's complaints as follows:

> By this time he was very confused by the whole situation. He had been denied access to a solicitor. No one would beleive (*sic*) his innocence and he could not understand why Bell and Latimer were 'going Queen's evidence'. Physically he was weak and tired ... A new suggestion was made to him. It came from Detective [Gerard] Walsh and it was that he would write a statement for him but 'it wouldn't be murder' ... At Interview No. 20 ... Detective Inspector [Edward Joseph] Garvey entered ... Hegan thought that he might believe his innocence and he asked to see him alone. The two detectives left the room. The inspector told him ... to 'distance' himself from Latimer and Bell and that a statement could be made that 'would not mean murder' and that he would get four years. When When (*sic*) the inspector asked should he get [Robert Alexander] Orr and [Gerard] Walsh back, Hegan nodded his head.
>
> There was then a discussion ... He was told Latimer and Bell would be pleading guilty and ... Detective Inspector [Edward Joseph] Garvey said he could put the blame on Bell and Latimer in the statement and that he (Hegan) thought they had been involved in terrorist activity ...[29]

Hegan maintains this statement, Exhibit 13 was induced by

the combination of ill-treatment and by promises made to him. Later offers to go supergrass were made if he could tell other names and say where the weapon came from.[30] The police denied all improprieties.

The judge dismissed Hegan's pleas as a catalogue of lies. After all, he was a soldier, able to sustain such pressure. Yet are we to accept that all soldiers are as suggested by the media and the popular press as being super-strong resilient heroes able to withstand degrees of pain and pressure unthinkable to the civilian? In my view this assumption would have validity if the case was against trained SAS soldiers who undergo such resistance training as part of their basic training. But he was dealing with UDR soldiers, only one of whom had three years full-time experience. As outlined earlier Hegan claimed that threats were made to him and his family and on this basis he made the incriminating statements. The judge found it as fact that he had not been subjected to such pressure. To this day Hegan maintains he was.

The fourth man convicted, Winston Allen, maintains that he too was mistreated by his interrogators until he felt forced to compromise his position by telling lies that he believed would distance himself from Latimer and the others whom he now believed had confessed openly to the murder of Adrian Carroll. In December 1983, Allen was questioned along with the others by the SIB (Special Investigation Bureau – part of the military police who investigate internal matters) at Drumadd Barracks concerning the murder charge, and released because there was no evidence against him. He was informed that the RUC would be making arrests in connection with this murder investigation of UDR members. Allen was therefore aware that he would be brought in for questioning as a routine procedure. He had the details of the day in question refreshed in his mind and was prepared for the impending arrest that he was aware would soon come.

His first interview at Castlereagh was relaxed and informal. Allen gave the police the details of his duties on that day to the interrogating officers. During the trial and *Voir Dire* concerning the admissibility of the police evidence against Allen he alleged that the police then turned on him, insulted him and claimed that he had told a parcel of lies.[31] Allen was shocked by the u-turn in the police officers' attitude. Allen claims that from then on the interviews became aggressive and hostile with the interrogators insisting on their version of events until Allen felt compelled to agree. Allen claimed that he felt shocked and degraded by the verbal abuse. Throughout the whole episode the detectives maintained one line of questioning, namely that his landrover stopped at Lonsdale Street to make a mock-arrest. Allen was aware that it was possible for the landrovers to have passed Lonsdale Street on their journey back to base. He said 'I compromised to their lies and I said Bell had got out of the Rover', meaning at Lonsdale Street. He thought that this would 'take them off his back for a while' ...[32] Allen then found himself in a confusing maze. At the trial it was put to the police that they knew Allen was a 'softie' and that by shouting at him he would break down.[33] The police deny all allegations of impropriety in the manner that he was interviewed but did admit that they shouted at Allen. The judge accepted their explanation. Allen says differently – claiming that he made the incriminating statements in a confused state of mind. At the trial it was alleged that during his questioning Allen was pushed to the point where he broke down. A complaint against one of the officers was made for slapping Allen on the face during the interrogating sessions.[34] The trial judge ruled that no assault had taken place. Winston Allen claims he broke down into uncontrollable tears and shaking. The police claim that Allen made a verbal admission at an evening interrogation session. However, they did not go back for a written admission until the next day. The normal police practice in such circumstances is that the police strike while the iron is hot. They would not leave the detainee to sleep on what he had said, but would be eager to get that confession on paper. Allen's lawyers have consistently questioned the validity of this police claim. His solicitor brought to my attention an offer of a lesser charge that was made to Allen throughout the trial – if he admitted knowledge he would have been charged with a lesser offence. Allen refused this offer knowing he could walk free or receive a lesser sentence if he admitted guilt.[35] I believe this tells us something of the character of the man who if he admitted guilt would get a lesser charge and a shorter sentence and in effect would be out of jail now.

Allen claims that page after page of notes was taken down. At his trial his defence claimed Allen's written confession was a copy of a question and answer session made from these police notes.[36] This was not accepted by the courts. Allen said he felt trapped throughout his time at Castlereagh. No one would believe his innocence despite his protests. Allen's claim is that he was trapped by his own confession and the belief that the system would not prosecute him on such absurd nonsense. He wanted to believe the police were going to help him and were his friends. Allen began to fear that something wrong and illegal had happened that day in Armagh. He started to believe that he had been made part of a murder plot without even knowing, and he confessed he felt brainwashed. Colin Worton, the soldier against whom charges were dropped, claimed in a radio interview that 'they sort of play on you ... I was really thinking you know that we had done it like, eventually ... its like a brainwashing thing' – this is the same kind of pressure that Allen, along with the others, claim they were subjected to.

Throughout the police interrogation the accused maintain they were mentally brought to a point where they believed in their own guilt. For each of them the whole situation appeared insurmountable. A question of doubt was placed in their own minds by the suggestion that each had been involved in a plot to a greater or lesser degree, some unaware of the full implications of their own position. If, as the men say, this is true, it is clear why each man wanted to distance himself from the gunman who, they were all told, was Latimer. Once Witness A's statement was available, the emphasis in the police investigation had switched from a stolen Cortina car that pointed to a Belfast connection to the involvement of the local UDR patrol. This gave them a pattern to follow. Once the men began to agree that the landrovers stopped in Lonsdale Street that element would have corroborated Witness A's statement. With Latimer breaking down and confessing, it appears to me that the police were then sure they had the right men. The three others allege each man was advised to distance themselves from Latimer.

This belief that the police interrogators were helping them placed them in jeopardy. They were under no obligation to make any statement yet they wanted to assist with the police enquiries if they could. After all, they were part of the security system. It was part and parcel of their nature to assist the police and not to take the option of remaining silent. If the UDR Four are the killers then they are naive in the extreme – as they apparently believed the RUC would not prosecute the case with vigour. One explanation is the four convicted were the four weak links out of the twenty odd soldiers arrested and questioned by the police. The police had been keen to press charges against other members of the platoon.

Why this particular army unit? Was it just a case of bad luck or does the answer lie with Witness A? If the police brief was based upon unreliable evidence and the confessions based on that evidence then the credibility of the conviction is under question and the case against the UDR Four collapses.

6

Witness A

In his judgment and sentence Lord Justice Basil Kelly stated that the UDR men involved in the murder of Adrian Carroll, 'devised a clever little charade to avert suspicion'.[1] That charade was the mock-arrest of Latimer by his UDR colleagues in Lonsdale Street. Lord Justice Kelly refers to this as the 'central feature of this game'.[2] The overriding question about this murder plot is, why did they go to such lengths of a mock-arrest in an attempt to avert suspicion and appear normal when in reality these men were drawing attention to themselves by such an act? If, as Lord Justice Kelly says, the mock-arrest is central to this game, then it is reasonable to assume that it is given full consideration in any examination of the UDR Four case and exposed as either a true or false reflection of what took place in Armagh on 8 November 1983.

The confessions and statements made by the four accused are built around the 'charade' of a mock-arrest in Lonsdale Street. The reason why this is a central feature of the prosecution case is that it is the only corroboration the prosecution has for the police evidence on Latimer. The prosecution case is based upon the premise that they have a key eye-witness who saw Neil Latimer wearing similar garb as that worn by the gunman. Necessity for the truth insists that this witness' account is fully examined.

Witness A was the principal player in the case against Neil Latimer and others versus the crown. Her testimony was used to establish the guilt of Latimer, and by association Bell, Hegan and Allen. When every avenue and parameter of her testimony is examined, gaping inconsistencies and what counsel for the defence described as blatant lies are revealed. The crown conceded that the cross-examination of Witness A revealed that she was not completely accurate in her account of how she came to make her original statement to Fr Murray. She was wrong in giving the time of the television broadcast in which she claimed the description of the murderer was given. She was inconsistent on points of detail concerning the mock-arrest. For instance in relation to the amount of soldiers involved, the existence of back doors on the UDR vehicles and the colour of the duffle coat worn as a disguise. She undoubtedly hedged about admitting a previous conviction for larceny in 1967 – a conviction that would not be easily forgotten. Lord Justice Kelly acknowledged these defects in her evidence and said of her cross-examination:

> Their cross-examinations of Mrs A did reveal inconsistencies i (sic) her evidence, mistakes, some faulty recollections, some contradictions, some inconsistencies between her evidence in court and what she had said in ehr (sic) statements to Father Murray and to the police.[3]

Having considered these discrepancies, mistakes and inconsistencies which defence counsel described as lies the trial judge concluded that they were peripheral. He said:

> ... Peripheral to the central feature she observed which was Latimer, a man she knew well, in civilian clothes yet a member of the UDR, wearing glasses which he normally did not, wearing a distinctive cap, Being run by fellow members of the UDR towards the back of a jeep. What she saw was most unusual. And it was puzzling. It must have rivetted her attention, probably to the detriment of the background features that surrounded it.[4]

Her credibility as a reliable witness has been called into

question from the very start of the case. This witness was not the sole crown witness who was called to give an eye-witness account of the events in Armagh that day. Elaine Faulkner was the key eye-witness and must be given careful consideration. She saw the gunman moments before Adrian Carroll was murdered. Her testimony is in juxtaposition to that of Witness A as she is adamant that the man she saw that day was definitely not Neil Latimer.

Both women knew Latimer. Faulkner lived in the same housing district and saw him on a regular basis. Witness A also knew Latimer as she had worked with him at a factory. Latimer, being a jocular sort of chap, never took much notice of her. During the trial Witness A on numerous occasions insisted that she knew Latimer well and 'I did not say he committed a murder. I did not see him commit a murder. In fact I don't think he committed a murder. In fact I do not think he is capable of doing that'.[5] Here there existed the ludicrous situation where the primary crown witness whose evidence was used to point the finger of blame at these four men, believed that the man she saw was innocent of the crime he was convicted of. These confusing and strange episodes must be sifted to arrive at the truth, and the out-come must balance one woman's credibility and word against another's.

Witness A, who chose to remain anonymous throughout the trial, made a formal statement to a senior RUC officer on 2 December 1983. That was over three weeks after Carroll was murdered. (This statement was finally arrived at after other meetings had taken place. The original statement was probably given around 22 November.) In her statement on 2 December she claimed she was privy to a strange event in Lonsdale Street shortly before Carroll was murdered. She claimed she left her home around four o'clock with her son and drove the short distance to Armagh to do some messages in the town centre. She drove first to the post office in College Street where her son carried out her business for her at the post office. On his return to the car she gave him money to buy a record. He was away for about ten minutes. Witness A remembers driving down Lonsdale Street, 'the traffic was just usual for that time of the evening'.[6] As she drove down Lonsdale Street she claims she:

> saw a UDR landrover parked at an angle across the road in front of me ... The tail of the landrover was facing the railings at the Technical School. The landrover had its full lights on. As I approached the landrover I slowed down and stopped only a short distance away from it. I would not have been more than a car length from the landrover. There was no way I could get past because of the way the landrover was parked.[7]

Witness A stopped believing there was a bomb scare or that there had been a shooting. She stopped thinking that she would be asked to reverse out of the way. However, none of the UDR soldiers paid any 'particular attention' to her presence.[8] Witness A then claimed that:

> My attention was then drawn to the steps between the main Technical School building and the Portacabin. I saw two UDR soldiers and a civilian come down these steps running. The civilian was in the middle and the soldiers were on each side of him. Both soldiers were carrying rifles. The civvy had his hands in his jacket pockets. They all had their heads down at this stage and I immediately thought they had arrested him.[9]

Witness A then goes on to say that they looked up and then:

> I immediately recognised the one in civilian clothes as Neil Latimer. He was wearing a tartan cap and wearing glasses. He was wearing what looked to me to be a brown coloured anorak or rain coat. When I saw Neil it was the glasses that drew my attention. They looked funny on him. They were gold rimmed and appeared to be too small for him.[10]

Witness A then claims she saw two soldiers and Latimer climb aboard the waiting landrover. As she knew Latimer and knew he was a UDR soldier she claims she thought the situation confusing and believed Latimer was probably getting married and his colleagues were 'taking him away to do him up'.[11] She thought nothing more about what she had seen and began her homeward journey with her son.

As she prepared dinner that evening her daughter arrived home and told her that one of the Carrolls had been shot. She claimed that she remembered listening to the news later that evening:

> Around 9 pm that evening I again listened to the news on BBC1 and it mentioned the shooting and the fact the fellow had died in hospital. It then gave a description of the gunman involved. They said he was small build with hair turning grey, wearing a brown jacket and tartan cap and wearing glasses ... Immediately I connected the description with that of what I had seen Neil Latimer wearing earlier that evening at the UDR landrovers in Lonsdale Street. I was completely shocked ... I didn't know what to do.[12]

This witness did nothing for one week. She claims she kept turning the thing over in her mind until she felt she had to talk to someone.[13] The person she talked to was a priest from Armagh, Fr Raymond Murray.[14] During the trial she claimed she visited Fr Murray at the Parochial House in Armagh, and, to her surprise, Fr Denis Faul was present, but said nothing to her. Fr Murray, on hearing what she had to say, told her it was a police matter. Witness A was cross-examined by Tony Cinnamond QC on this point:

> Q. Was the entire interview conducted at the parochial house?
> A. I made a statement there, yes.
> Q. And after having made that statement you left?
> A. That's right ... I did.
> Q. ... And the only two people present when that statement was made was yourself and Father Murray ... I'm talking

about the statement you made to Father Murray in the parochial house.

A. There was another priest there with him.

Q. There was another priest there with him. Who was that?

A. Father Fall *(sic)*.

Q. Father Fall *(sic)* from Dungannon?

A. Yes.

Q. Did Father Fall *(sic)* just happen to be there?

A. I don't know.

Q. Well of course Father Murray didn't know you were going to call round that morning, isn't that right?

A. No.

Q. ... Roughly when you got to see him, were you in sort of one room and ---

A. Yes. In one room with a big table ... Father Murray came in, Father Fall *(sic)* came in a short time later ... 25 minutes. I can't remember.

Q. And you told your story to them, did you?

A. I told Father Murray.

Q. Did you not tell it to Father Fall *(sic)* also?

A. He didn't really ask me anything ...

Q. And after you told this story, did Father Murray then take a statement from you?

A. He did.

Q. Well how did he take it?

A. He just said he thought it was a matter for the police

Q. Yes, but how did he take it ... did he write it out or type it or what?

A. He wrote it out. ...

Q. Did he get you to sign the written statement?

A. Yes.

Q. ... So is it right to say that you never signed a typewritten statement for Fr Murray?

A. Not typed; it was written ...

...

Q. Did you sign any blank sheets of paper for Father Murray?

A. I did.

Q. Oh, you did?

A. Yes.

Q. That's the first we have heard about this ... Where did you sign these blank sheets of paper?

A. In my own house. He came to my house.

Q. Why did he want you to sign blank sheets of paper?
A. I presumed he was going to type in that statement on different sheets of paper.
Q. You have never seen a typed statement from Father Murray, have you?
A. No ....

...

Q. How many sheets did you sign?
A. Seven or eight. I can't remember.[15]

Three days later – the exact dates are unclear –the police took a written statement from her at Raymond Murray's house.[16] She claims she was told she would not be a witness and her son would not be called to give evidence at any trial. The police then took Witness A to Lonsdale Street where maps were drawn to assist with enquiries, with Witness A's claims superimposed on the map.[17] It is unlikely that we can accept many of Witness A's accusations based upon her inability to state the facts in a lucid manner.

After these series of interviews a number of arrests of UDR soldiers took place.The statement Witness A proceeded to make on 2 December was to gather all the loose ends together and finalise things. At no time does it appear that the police actually questioned the validity of the accusations being made, but accepted her statement as a *prima facie* case to be answered. It was after this series of events that Latimer was arrested on 29 November 1983 from his house in Lisnally Gardens, Armagh.

When the case came for trial in February 1986, Witness A was to play a prominent role. The prosecution maintain the mock-arrest is central to the overall plot to kill Adrian Carroll.[18] The prosecution case relies upon the thesis that 'the plan to commit this murder was premeditated and clever. It was carried out by the accused during the course of their duties as soldiers in Armagh and that fact was used as a means and as a cover to commit the murder ... The reason for dropping Latimer off at the college was to enable him to change from uniform into civilian clothes ...'[19] It was imperative that the confessions concentrated around the events in Lonsdale Street. During cross-examination Witness A's statement was proved to be riddled with flaws. When studying the transcripts of the trial and in particular the testimony of Witness A, a sense of unreality is apparent. Her mental ability to recall events accurately and lucidly is beyond doubt, absent. She was obviously confused and her memory clouded beyond recognition at times. Throughout her cross-examination this point is underlined:

Q. And let us get this clear, you have known Neil Latimer quite a while?
A. Yes, and he is a very nice fellow.
Q. I think that is the second time that you have said that.
A. Well I am very fond of him. He has done nothing on me.
Q. Are you trying to impress my Lord that you are very impartial and that you are an objective sort of witness by saying that you like Neil Latimer?
A. He was quite good when I worked with him.
Q. Do you still like Neil Latimer?
A. Yes I do.
Q. But you think he committed a murder, don't you?
A. I did not say he committed a murder. I did not see him commit a murder. In fact I don't think he committed a murder. In fact I do not think he is capable of doing that ... I do not think he is that type of fellow at all ... The fact is I did not see him doing it so I cannot accuse him of doing anything. I did not see him doing it.
Q. It never crossed your mind that he committed a murder?
A. No ...
Q. I will be giving you an opportunity of answering that question again. Do you say that it never crossed your mind that he committed a murder?
A. The only thing that crossed my mind was the description on the news of the clothes being worn (... description of the tartan cap, brown anorak, glasses) ...
Q. So you said to yourself, did you: 'Oh, Neil Latimer must have been the gunman'?
A. No, I didn't.
Q. You didn't. What did you say to yourself?

A. I said he fitted the description of the man that was seen running away from the scene of the shooting.

Q. ... Well, the person running away from the scene of the shooting would be likely to be a gunman, isn't that right?

A. That's right.

Q. Well, did you not say to yourself: 'Well it must have been Neil Latimer who was the gunman'?

A. After a time. After a week I thought about it.

Q. Why did it take a week?

A. I didn't report anything for about a week ... I couldn't be sure ...

Q. It took you a week to come to that conclusion?

A. It did ....

Q. It took you a week to come to the conclusion that the man whom it was said was seen running away from the scene was Neil Latimer?

A. That's right.

Q. ... Would you please explain to My Lord how it could possibly have taken one week for you to come to that conclusion?

A. I thought about it a lot and it started annoying me then. I didn't go to the police, I mentioned it to Father Murray first ... I couldn't sleep with it on my head ... Each time I closed my eyes I could see them three people running dressed in them clothes, and it kept annoying me ... It took me a week to pick up the courage to go and tell somebody what I had seen at the technical college...

Q. Did you tell the police at some stage ...'Immediately I connected the description with that of what I had seen Neil Latimer wearing earlier that evening at the UDR Landrovers in Lonsdale Street'?

A. True. But I couldn't be absolutely sure it was the same man.[20]

Witness A had a sincere sense of believing what she said one moment and then denying the context and meaning of her words the next. As long as she can reconcile events, 'in my own mind' and 'as I see it' then she could change the meanings of her words, phrases and statements.[21] Her credibility as a reliable witness became questionable on numerous occasions when confronted about the truthfulness of her statement and how it came about. On Wednesday 5 March 1986 she went over her statement for the court. It was only then that Father Murray's role in the events came to light. The trial was adjourned on Monday 10 March in order to facilitate defence requests to examine Father Murray's material. When Witness A was recalled she then changed her version of events and claimed she could not remember what had happened and what she had said clearly on the previous Wednesday. Neither could she remember clearly how she came to make her original statement to the priest in the first place:

> Q. I am talking about the statement which you made and made to Father Murray.
> A. I cannot be clear about that.
> Q. You cannot be clear about that at all?
> A. Not absolutely clear.
> Q. Yet last week you were prepared to sit in the witness box and swear that a certain sequence of events had taken place?
> A. I told the thing as it came to me. I told it as it came to my mind and as I remembered it or tried to remember it.
> Q. And it (*sic*) may or may not have been true?
> A. As far as I can remember waht (*sic*) I told was true. I have tried to tell the truth as I seen things ... What I said about Father Murray may not have been 100 per cent as to the circumstances in which I met him ...
> Q. Why didn't you tell us last week you were confused about it?
> A. I had to think about it over the week end ...
> Q. You knew that in the meantime we might check up on matters that might prove you wrong?
> A. It never entered my head that you would check matters ...
> Q. I suggest that you changed your evidence from telling my lord last week quite clearly what happened to the point where you are not sure ....[22]

All she could tell the court was 'that's the picture as I saw it.'[23] She would not share those clear thoughts with the court.

On Wednesday 5 March, Witness A told the court that

she had phoned Fr Murray one week after Carroll was murdered. Unable to speak to Fr Murray on the phone, she then on chance called at Fr Murray's house.[24] It was there that she met him and made her statement in order to get the load off her mind. Fr Faul was present throughout, but because he said nothing Witness A claimed he had no relevance to the conversation. Asked if she had contacted or tried to contact Fr Faul she said, 'no definitely not'.

On Monday 10 March 1986 she claimed that Fr Murray came to her house after she had phoned him, and that she later signed blank sheets of paper for him. It is unclear what significance, if any, this has. Fr Faul is on record as saying that she signed the typed version of the statement. In an article in the *Irish News*, 4 December 1990, Fr Faul said:

> ... it insinuates malpractice to say the woman waited for a fortnight, as if she had concocted the whole story, and then had got the two priests to join in the concoction.
>
> Everything she did was honourable, and she acted as urgently as she could, and everything the priests did in connection with the statement was honourable and above board.

She also remembered going to Fr Murray's house to meet him and Fr Faul. Witness A then went back on the Fr Faul meeting and accepted after much argument that she had phoned Directory Enquiries on more than one occasion in an attempt to contact Fr Faul. Then in an outburst to the court she said Latimer could not have carried out the murder: 'In fact I don't think he committed a murder. In fact I do not think he is capable of doing that ... I do not think he is that type of fellow at all.'[25] When asked why she went to Fr Murray and not her own priest she said that 'Murray dealt with this sort of thing' referring to complaints against the UDR. Yet she contradicted this statement time and time again, assuring the court that she had no complaint against the UDR. In another burst of impartiality she said that the UDR were doing 'a good job'.[26] Questioned on why it took her so long to go to the police with her statement Witness A said that it had taken her time to add up the significance and meaning of what she had seen. Yet in her police statement she said she immediately 'connected the description (of the gunman on BBC) with that of what I had seen Neil Latimer wearing earlier that evening ...[27]

In reality, it was approximately two weeks after Carroll was murdered before Witness A featured in the case. It was Witness A, the prosecution's trump card, who later claimed that the 'whole case has never been right from the start'.[28] It is this that casts doubt upon the validity and truthfulness of any and all of her claims.

Both in her statement and in court Witness A claimed that she heard a description of the gunman on BBC television news at 9 o'clock on the evening Carroll was murdered. A compete study of the BBC and UTV news transcripts for that day prove this statement as false. Witness A's statement was taken she claimed, after she had identified Latimer from a description on television. The fact that no description was ever played on television raises serious doubts about the truth of her statement and how she got access to this material. On 5 March 1986 she told the court:

> ... I think it was BBC 1 ...
> Q. And what description did you hear?
> A. Description of the tartan cap, brown anorak, glasses.[29]

The following Monday in court, Witness A had to concede that this was wrong:

> Q. Isn't the truth of the matter that that this is a bundle of untruths ... ?
> A. Oh, no, what I seen I've told what I've seen and that's the truth. I certainly didn't set about to tell lies, because I never wanted to get involved in the first place ... I wouldn't deliberately tell a lie to any Court.
> Q. Mrs A it would appear to be the situation that neither the

BBC television or the UTV television broadcast on the night
of the 8th any description of the man who was seen running
away from the scene or any other man connected with the
murder?

A. As far as I can remember they did ...

Q. Haven't you just been painting for my Lord an extremely
detailed picture of how you were sitting in the living room,
with the lights on close to the television and then this
description came on, you believe, the 9 o'clock news on, you
believe, BBC 1, and your son turned round to you and said
words to the effect 'That's the man we saw' and you said
words to the effect 'That's Neil Latimer'?

A. That's correct ...

Q. ... Are you saying beyond a doubt that that description was
given?

A. It was, as far as I can remember.

Q. Have you any difficulty remembering this?

A. The news?

Q. Yes, the news.

A. No, I can remember sitting listening to the news ... I still
say the description was given. As far as I am concerned the
description was given on the news ... the nine o'clock news.[30]

Witness A went on asserting that she had heard this description despite proof to the contrary. In a report in the
Belfast Telegraph the day after Carroll was shot it stated
the police were looking for 'a man who wore a tartan hat
and a brown duffle coat. He was of medium build with grey
hair'. This description of the gunman was incorrect. In the
official RUC statement it claimed the man they wished to
question was '5'1" or 5'2", slim medium build, mid length
neat, straight dirty fair hair, light moustache, small
squinty eyes. Wearing a blue and grey large check or tartan
patterned cap with plain cloth peak, a light blue duffle
coat, light weight shoes and gold rim glasses. The *Belfast
Telegraph* account was wrong on the colour of the coat and
the physique of the man. Yet Witness A maintained the
description contained the brown duffle coat. If it could be
shown she was unreliable concerning how she came across
this description of the gunman surely her ability to re-

collect accurately about events in Lonsdale Street in November 1983 must also be questioned.

Again on 10 March a parcel of inconsistencies in her evidence became apparent. Witness A claimed that she saw the back doors of the landrovers, then later on she denied seeing the back doors of the landrovers at all. In her statement to Fr Murray (typed version) she said, 'Then they all got into the Land Rover ... he got in with the first one, the one blocking me .... It paused a minute until back doors and all were closed'.[31] However during cross-examination she then went back on this point of detail, she said:

> Q. And did you say ... 'and then they all got into the Land Rover...it paused a minue *(sic)* until back doors and all were closed' ... Did you tell that to Father Murray?
> A. I cannot remember whether I talked about the back. I saw them getting in.
> Q. Why pick on the back doors ...?
> A. Because I could not see the doors. I could not have seen the doors. From the position I was in ...
> Q. Well why did you tell Father Murray that the back doors were closed? ... Why did you pick on the issue of the back doors ...?
> A. ... I cannot remember seeing the back doors.
> Q. Do you know the next question which is coming? ... Has anyone discussed with you the whether or not there are back doors on U.D.R. Land Rovers in Armagh?
> A. No. No one has ever said anything about back doors in Land Rovers.
> Q. So you are honestly telling the court that when you gave these answers that you have given and picked on the back doors out of the sentence that I have read to you that you did not know the U.D.R. Land Rovers in Armagh had no back doors?
> A. I didn't know anything about back doors and I am not acquainted with it at all. I see them from time to time but I do not look closely at them. I do not go out of my way to look at them and I could not have seen the doors from the situation I was in.[32]

At another juncture she told the court that she saw four soldiers crouched at each wheel of the landrover. She later changed this to only being able to see two soldiers. By the end of her statement she had too many soldiers crammed into the back of one landrover. On other points concerning whether or not the lights of the landrovers were on or off, Witness A was again found to be mistaken.[33]

Witness A was then questioned about her credibility as a reliable and truthful witness. Claiming that she was indeed both truthful and upright she denied she had ever been in court before for anything major. This was proved to be a total misrepresentation of the truth. Mr Weir cross-examined Witness A on 11 March 1986. During his cross-examination the following was revealed:

Q. You have never appeared in Court?
A. Not on anything major, a motoring offence or something like that ....
Q. But apart from motoring things, never anything?
A. Not that I can recall, no ...
Q. You don't remember being in Court for anything other than motoring offences?
A. No ...
Q. ... Were you convicted of any offence, not your son, not your family, you?
A. I was fined £10 and I could never understand the reason why...
Q. What were you fined £10 for when you landed at Court with your son?
A. Because they tried to make it appear that I was connected with it ...
Q. It looks as if they were fairly successful?
A. Sometimes they are but they are not always correct.
Q. That seems to have occurred on this occasion that you are describing?
A. That's years ago.
Q. Just tell my Lord straightforwardly now that you are confronted with it, what was it?
A. A pound of butter. They connected me with a pound of butter.
Q. And they fined you, did they?

A. £10.

Q. Why did you not say that?

A. I never lifted any butter or anything like that. As far as I am concerned I was innocent.

Q. As far as you are concerned today you are telling the truth?

A. I am.

Q. The point I'm putting to you is that you were convicted of stealing?

A. I was convicted of lifting one pound of butter.

Q. I don't care if it was a pound of butter or a diamond ring, you were convicted of stealing?

A. In there I was, yes, but I know in my own mind I didn't do it.

Q. Don't you know in your own mind that you saw nothing in Lonsdale Street that afternoon?

A. I know in my own mind what I did see. [34]

This woman misled the court about her past. In 1967 she was found guilty of stealing. In an effort to overcome her lies she side-stepped the issue stating that in 'her mind' she was not the one guilty but it was her son who was with her at the time, claiming that it remained a mystery to her why she was ever fined. Despite these inconsistencies which should have destroyed any credible fibre that the witness claimed to possess, Lord Justice Basil Kelly accepted the essential part of her testimony about Lonsdale Street as a true and reliable account of what took place. Why was Elaine Faulkner not given the same treatment? Her testimony was accurate and lucid yet the basis of it, namely that Latimer was definitely not the gunman, was ignored.

Examining the testimony of Elaine Faulker as compared to that of Witness A makes for interesting conclusions. Unlike Witness A there was no inconsistency or hesitation in her evidence. She was the crown witness who was able to identify the gunman and give a description to the police shortly after the shooting took place. Elaine Faulkner is the most prominent and important witness, as she alone saw the gunman moments before the shooting took place.

Elaine Faulkner worked in Dawson Street which is just above Abbey Street in Armagh. On 8 November 1983 she went to Abbey Street post office. As she finished posting letters in the post box at the bottom of Abbey Street she turned and saw a man walk past her. In any other circumstances she would have taken little notice, but moments later this same man, who had been less than one foot away from her, pulled a gun from his coat as he darted down the entry where Adrian Carroll lived. The man was so close to her moments before that his features and details about his clothes fixed themselves in Elaine Faulkner's mind. He was a small man, probably only 5'1" or 5'2". Elaine Faulkner is 5'4" so he was smaller than her. He had a slim physique. His face was small and narrow and he had fair hair. He wore a checked or tartan peaked cap, gold rimmed spectacles and a light blue duffle coat.

On witnessing this man pull the gun from his coat, Faulkner froze with apprehension and fear. Seconds later she heard the shots that killed Adrian Carroll. She paused for a moment and then crossed to the other side of Abbey Street. She then ran back up the street towards her office. It is a narrow street and she did not see the gunman return or run past her on his way down the street. The only way that he could escape was to run up the street. When Faulkner got to her workplace she spoke to her employer about what she had just seen. He immediately took her to the police station where she made a full statement. Elaine Faulkner was certain that if she saw the man again she would recognise him.

During the trial she testified that she lived in the same housing estate as Latimer and knew him. When asked if Latimer was the gunman she was adamant it was not him. The judge rebuked the crown counsel for cross-examining his own witness on this point of Latimer's identification.[35] Physically Latimer did not match the description that Faulkner gave to the police. He is tall, about 5'10" and has dark, not fair, hair; neither did he have a moustache in 1983. Faulkner would have had the advantage of knowing Latimer and if it was he who had walked so close to her, would have acknowledged his presence with some sort of greeting. If Latimer was the gunman, Faulkner's presence would have been the greatest deterrent to him to carry out a murder. It would have been unspeakable folly for him to shoot Carroll with a neighbour looking on.

It was Elaine Faulkner's promptness that furnished the police with a photo-fit of the killer within an hour of the shooting. It only took her twenty minutes to take her evidence to the police, unlike Witness A who waited as long as a fortnight to report. The credibility and acceptability of these two divergent testimonies must be placed in the balance of truth. The overall character and demeanour of Witness A loses credibility when compared to those same characteristics of Elaine Faulkner's. The assumption by the judge that both witnesses were telling the truth, but that Elaine Faulkner was wrong about the identity of Latimer, is most baffling and disturbing.[36]

During the trial Witness A was recalled on 9 June 1986. It emerged that she had set aside legal protocol and had made contact with Noel Bell's mother:

Q. Did you telephone the mother of the defendant Bell on Thursday evening last?
A. I did.
Q. And did you ring her to her home?
A. I did.
Q. And you confirm to My Lord that you did that of your own initiative, that it was not as a result of a 'phone call from Mrs Bell to you or any approach by her?
A. Oh, no, no I did it myself.[37]

Witness A says she had become anxious over the case and made this approach to Mrs Bell the day after Colin Worton was discharged on the basis that his statement to the police had not been voluntary.

115

> Q. And did you mention the fact that you'd read in the papers
> how the accused had been tricked into making statements?
> A. That's right ...
> Q. What did you say about that to Mrs Bell?
> A. I wasn't pleased about that. I didn't believe the other boys
> made their statements either. I think if it applied in the case
> of one, it applied in the case of them all.
> Q. Did you say you were disgusted?
> A. I did.
> Q. And did you say to her that you realized that she'd been
> told -- that you'd been told lies by the police?
> A. I had been told on one occasion that they don't force
> anybody to make a statement if they don't make it of their
> own free will. And I mean it has been done there.[38]

Witness A says that she had made her statement to the police under certain conditions. Firstly, that another witness had seen Neil Latimer moments before the murder. As it turned out that other witness was Elaine Faulkner who said no such thing. Witness A gave her testimony believing the identity of the gunman was already known. The second condition was that the police had told her that they (the UDR) had 'made their own admissions', and her statement was just a matter of detail.[39]

Witness A then told Mrs Bell that she wished to have nothing to do with the affair, 'I believe the men are innocent, I've always believed that', and that she wished to retract her evidence.[40] This startling development was another blow to the credibility of the witness and to the crown case. The central pillar of the case was collapsing. Witness A demonstrably wanted to wash her hands of the whole affair which was in her own words 'not right from the start'. However Witness A did not and has not retracted the most important aspects of her statement, namely that she saw Latimer in civilian clothes being mock-arrested. The important point is whether or not this witness can be believed. In a recorded telephone conversation with Tom Hegan (James Hegan's father), Witness A alleged an unidentified member of the RUC drove her to Portadown and spoke bluntly concerning the consequences of any retraction. There follows an extract from a telephone conversation Witness A had on 17 August of 1990 with Tom Hegan concerning why she would not retract all of her evidence:

> A. He (the policeman) didn't say very much. I told him I was going down to retract everything I wasn't satisfied with it. They told me that them boys if they got out would kill all round them. That they were bad boys and that no judge in the land would ever let them out. He says that if they get out and they kill someone, he says, it will be your fault for letting them out ... because they'll murder all 'round them. I said I didn't believe they done it. He said, 'They done it all right'. So what d' you want me to ... what do you expect me to believe?
> H. Who said that to you?
> A. Police ...
> A. They definitely ... He said 'This is not the only thing', he said, 'they have been involved in a lot of other serious crimes we can't go into them ... we can't talk about it to you' he said
> ...
> ... I was available but. They knew that, I had told them to come for me within half an hour and I was ready here. I told them I was ready but he didn't come for me, he sent somebody else for me and said, 'you're not going to court you're going to Portadown', and I says, 'well what am I going to Portadown for?' He says, 'well I don't know dear', he says 'I'm just taking instructions from the top, that's the orders I got'.[41]

In an RTE interview with journalist Brendan Wright, Witness A explained her position. During the course of the interview it emerged that her position had altered considerably:

> I have been to hell and back if you like. This is for a reason ... I believe now that the police made a blunder ... and I think it is up to them to come up with the truth, not me ... The detectives at one stage told me they already knew who the murderer was and I asked them who it was and they said it

was Neil Latimer. And I said well how do you know it was Neil Latimer? He said because we already have another witness that was on the scene and made a statement directly after the killing ... and she had said it was Neil Latimer and she got a good look at him ... and she recognized him because she only lived around the corner. Now that turns out that its not true. It was very unfair that statement. I think they have tricked me. I see it as tricks ... dirty tricks department. I don't care how they see it ... none of them have approached me, but as far as I can see this girl has denied that ...that she ever gave his name. In fact she said that it wasn't him she seen. I mean whose telling lies?[42]

Upon these statements can the evidence of this witness still be considered credible? When such a parcel of ambiguities has been introduced, is it even possible to untangle the mess of inconsistencies and untruths? An official effort to ignore the context and content of her statements and play down not only its significance but the role of the witness herself has been made. In a reply from the then Secretary of State, Mr Tom King MP, to Lord Mason concerning this apparent retraction the Secretary of State claimed:

A transcription of the radio interview with Witness A has been carefully examined and it is clear that she has not retracted any of the evidence [that] was important only insofar as it linked one of the 4 UDR soldiers with the murder. This led to his interrogation by the police and the subsequent arrest of Mr Hegan and the others.[44]

The Secretary of State then goes on to move the goal posts and claims the witness is not at all important, neither does he consider her to be discredited in any way.

It is clear from the Appeal Court judgement that the main evidence against the accused was their confessions which were sufficient for a conviction even if Witness A had been discredited, which she was not.

I can find no grounds to justify my making a referrence of this case to the Court of Appeal.[44]

Such a curt reply only helped fuel accusations that an official cover-up has been going on since the convictions in July 1986. Obvious blunders, lies and accusations by a crown witness pass unchecked. Ian Stewart MP, an ex-Minister of State, reiterated the point to Peter Robinson in a letter dated 24 July 1989:

> ... even if Witness A's evidence was discredited, which it was note, *(sic)* there was sufficient other evidence to secure the convictions.
> I am afraid that until such time as new and substantial evidence is produced there are no grounds to justify referral of the case back to the Court of Appeal.[45]

The case without Witness A is hollow. Witness A was the prosecution's trump card for placing the blame on the UDR soldiers. The alleged statements by the accused are based upon her statement and are corroborated solely by Witness A and her alone. In my view to carry on this conviction with such distorted evidence would be a mutilation of justice. The implications that the Witness A episode raises are severe. Consider a situation where four young Catholic men are convicted for a murder they claim to know nothing about. The evidence used to convict them came from an unnamed witness, but through the channels of a Protestant minister or Unionist politician. Consider further the implications if that go-between was renowned for his vilification of the Republican community. Would such evidence gathering be considered credible in this suspicious and recriminating society?

Other new evidence has been given to the Secretary of State.[46] If these developments since the trial prove that this witness is unreliable, then her story and the confessions and statements, that the police claim to have been made without duress, were based upon a poor foundation.

An alternative and more plausible interpretation of the events was apparent throughout the trial, yet was brushed aside. This alternative points the finger at the real killer of Adrian Carroll.

James Hegan *(Pacemaker)*

Neil Latimer *(Pacemaker)*

Winston Allen *(Pacemaker)*

Noel Bell *(Pacemaker)*

Adrian Carroll *(Pacemaker)*

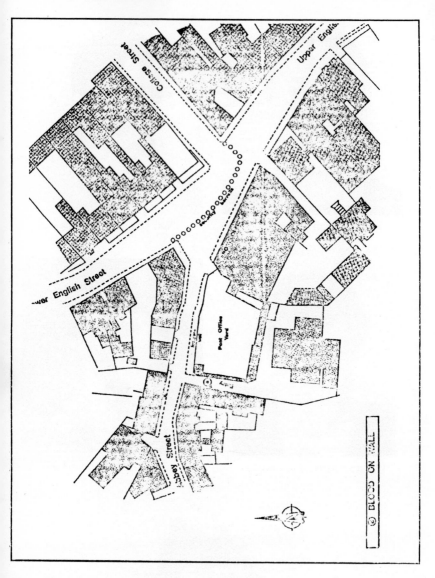

Map of area of Carroll shooting

Armagh Technical College

Alleyway off Abbey Street where Adrian Carroll was murdered
(from opposite directions)

Top: Looking up Abbey Street – this is where the gunman walked past Elaine Faulkner.

Bottom: Looking down Abbey Street – to the right is the alleyway where Adrian Carroll was murdered.

Stolen Ford Cortina abandoned at Market Place

Raymond Murray *(Pacemaker)*

Basil Kelly *(Pacemaker)*

Denis Faul *(Pacemaker)*

Sir John Hermon *(Pacemaker)*

James Prior *(Pacemaker)*

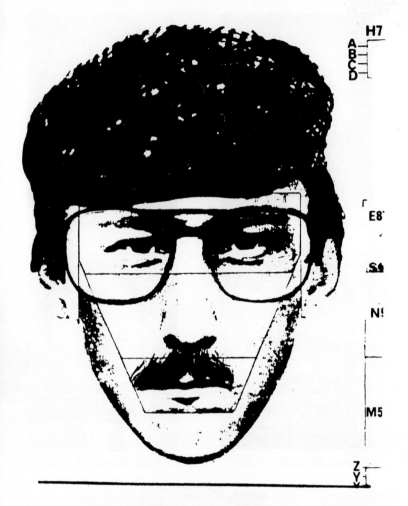

Photofit description given by Elaine Faulkner: Ref No. M.O. 205/83 dated 9.11.1983. Man wanted in connection with the Murder of Adrian Carroll in an entry off Abbey St., Armagh about 4.35pm on 8.11.83. AGE: 20-25 yrs, 5'1-2", slim/medium build, mid length neat straight dirty fair hair, light moustache, small squinty eyes, thin nose, small face and pale complexion. Wearing a blue and grey large check or tartan patterned cap with plain cloth peak and side panels, light blue duffel coat, light weight casual shoes and gold metal framed spectacles.

7

The PAF

As the relatives of Adrian Carroll mourned his passing on 8 November 1983, they must have had little hope that the killer of their son would be found, and justice done. The immediate police investigations highlighted the theory of how, why and who shot Adrian Carroll. The official leads that evening fell into three categories. Firstly, the ballistics evidence which could be extracted from Carroll's remains and traced to a particular weapon with exacting detail. Secondly, eye-witness accounts by three people. The primary eye-witness who gave a detailed description of the gunman to the RUC twenty minutes after Adrian Carroll was killed. Elaine Faulkner was the only person to see the gunman literally moments before the bullets were fired.

Another witness was Mrs Hegan, resident of 12 Abbey Street, who heard the footsteps as he ran away from Carroll's front door up Abbey Street in the direction of Cathedral Close. This witness, a neighbour of Adrian Carroll's, was in her house when she heard the shooting. Her young daughter was playing in the street outside and in a moment of panic the mother went out to get her child and ensure she was free from harm. Another crown witness, Mr Allen, the Archbishop's gardener who was carrying out routine repair work to the Cathedral garden, heard the gunshots. Moments later he saw two men speeding away from the scene of the murder, driving a dark blue Cortina car. This man testified to what he had seen.

The final evidence was the actual murder claim that evening to a local radio station. Terrorist organisations in

Northern Ireland use a method of recognised code words in order to authenticate claims. Chosen journalists and newspapers are privy to these buzz words. On hearing a code word, a radio station or newspaper can then establish the truth of the claim and tell the public and police who carried out a particular terrorist act.

Adrian Carroll's murder was no exception to this rule. Only a matter of hours later it was claimed by the Protestant Action Force who used a recognised and authenticated code-word claiming Carroll was a Republican and his Republican pedigree had singled him out for death. His brother, Roderick, was an active service INLA member who was ambushed and shot dead by an RUC counter-terrorist operation in December 1982. His other brother, Tommy Carroll, was a Sinn Féin councillor and was at the time a Sinn Féin election agent. Adrian Carroll's sympathy, latent or active, for the INLA and Republican movement was undoubted. Whether or not he was an actual serving member of a terrorist organisation is questionable. After all, he suffered from a hearing defect, rendering him a danger to any active service unit.

It seemed logically apparent that the murder of Adrian Carroll was another of the quota of sectarian killings that Northern Ireland has suffered over the past 20 years. If the UDR were going to carry out a 'hit' then they would choose a real target, after all their access to sound 'intelligence' would have helped them target an active IRA member. The RUC enquiry can only have used this circumstantial and material evidence to base their enquiries upon. Carroll was shot using a .38 Smith and Wesson revolver. One account has Carroll's assailant escaping by Cathedral Close, where the car was dumped and an alternative vehicle was used or else escaped by foot. The Cortina car pointed to a Belfast connection and had all the hallmarks of a typical sectarian killing. Ten to fourteen days later a complete turnaround in events sent the police enquiries in a totally different and somewhat ludicrous direction and brought members of the UDR to trial.

The original evidence and enquiry came to an end and a stampeding effort to forget that line and pursue a fresh one was effective. What is now necessary is that a full enquiry and examination of the alternative scenario is conducted, in a serious effort to confront the question *Who killed Adrian Carroll?* – keeping in mind that the conviction affects both the administration of justice in Northern Ireland, and the four men convicted.

According to the judgment of Lord Justice Basil Kelly, there was only one story given credibility. Any exploration or evidence that lent its weight to an alternative explanation became lost in his verdict. Lord Justice Kelly assumed UDR members were strong enough to resist any physical or verbal mistreatment while in Castlereagh, that security force members, being aware of the intricacies of their rights, would not allow themselves to be pressured into signing statements that were a deliberate perversion of the course of justice. Lord Justice Kelly assumed that some other soldiers who testified in defence of their colleagues were attempting an appalling exercise in covering over their colleagues' misdemeanours. He said that the key eye-witness, Elaine Faulkner, was 'totally wrong when she says that the man she saw produce a gun in Abbey Street was not the accused Latimer'.[1] The judge said that although Witness A's testimony was riddled with inconsistencies, 'the essential part of her evidence is true'. He further assumed that other testimonies and evidence that offered an alternative explanation for the murder, such as the gardener's eye-witness account of the Cortina car speeding away from the scene of the crime, the existence of forensic evidence surrounding the get-away vehicle, the testimony of Mrs Hegan, the Abbey Street resident and neighbour of Adrian Carroll, were all peripheral to the actual killing and thus without substantive weight to overrule the prosecution case. This evidence was brushed aside but, like pieces of a jigsaw puzzle when placed in order, put together a lucid and, in my opinion, more accurate account of what actually happened in Armagh on 8 November 1983. This alternative picture places the entirety of the blame for Adrian Carroll's murder on the outlawed terrorist organisation, the Protestant Action Force, and removes beyond the shadow of a doubt blame, even by association, on members of the UDR.

On Friday 6 April 1990, I received a telephone call inviting me to a meeting with a person who could point me in the direction of the killers of Adrian Carroll. I was instructed to drive to a destination on the Shankill Road where I was met. Around eight o'clock that evening, while waiting in the car discussing the various alternative options as to how the Carroll murder was carried out, a man jumped into the back of the car. He introduced himself as a member of the PAF who could speak as openly as circumstances would permit on evidence relating to the Carroll killing.

This man's identity was obviously concealed, but his authenticity as a PAF spokesman was confirmed by three sources, the first being political contacts who, having dealt with a UVF threat in the late 1970s on Maze prison officers, confirmed that this person was a member of the UVF Army Council who had negotiated the peaceful settlement of that dispute. The second source confirming his authenticity was the use of a code word that was later confirmed by a journalist who had dealt in the past with the organisation in question. The third was a police source who could identify the man, but for legal reasons I cannot reveal the identity of this senior RUC detective.

The man was in his late thirties and had an intricate and explicit knowledge of the case which was undoubtedly a demonstration to those present that he was in fact who he claimed to be. It came as no surprise that the PAF were involved in this murder. After all, on two occasions prior to this meeting the PAF issued press statements shedding light on the circumstances of Carroll's death and claiming responsibility for it. On the evening Carroll was shot, a local radio station confirmed that a coded message received from PAF sources claimed responsibility for the murder of Adrian Carroll. After the trial and conviction of Neil Latimer, Noel Bell, James Hegan and Winston Allen, it was almost four years before any other word from this source was received. On 13 September 1988 a PAF statement, breaking the silence in an effort to appease public pleas from the families that the real killers take the blame for the actions, was issued to the *News Letter* stating once again that the PAF carried out the murder of Adrian Carroll. Two other statements to the *Sunday World* on 19 November and 26 November 1989 again attempted to shed more light on these claims.

Such statements appeared to have little effect upon the authorities. However, they aroused serious attention from other quarters. In an effort to gain credibility for these claims, the PAF then made unprecedented moves by allowing its representative to speak to our committee members namely, Peter Robinson, Norman Bell, Robert Kee and myself. It was after these series of interviews that the major newspapers began to take interest in the claim.

The purpose of this meeting was for the PAF representative to shed light on the alternative scenario which was already the subject of much speculation. Certain rules of play were established from the outset. In no way would names of activists or information which could jeopardise the security of their people be released. This became clearer at a later stage of the talks when an attempt was made to establish the number of those involved in the Carroll murder – was it an individual, a two-man team, or a larger operation? In effect the contact could only give us a limited idea of the number involved.

How then was Adrian Carroll killed?

The intended target of the PAF was not Adrian Carroll. Active service units in Armagh had identified a 'renowned Republican gunman' who they claimed had been instrumental in serious crimes of genocide against the Protestant people. Although no name was mentioned, certain credentials pointed to this target's identity. He had served a time in the Maze for serious crimes and was, in 1983, just out of prison a few months. The Armagh operation followed this target and laid plans to kill him. Nine weeks before the shooting, the operation was passed through its Belfast operational command structure with a request for a vehicle and weapons and manpower to see this plot through.

On Thursday 8 September 1983 at around 11 am, Mrs Veronica Truesdale left her home in Argyle Street, Belfast, in her car, a midnight-blue Ford Cortina, 1300 cc, registration SOI 4596. She parked at Mountjoy Street, Shankill Road, Belfast where she then went about her shopping. Having visited two shops she returned and discovered her car was missing.[2] Mrs Truesdale was distressed and returned home. Along with her husband she reported the incident to the police. Two months afterwards that car was used in the murder of Adrian Carroll. Sometime in late December the Truesdales were permitted to recover the vehicle. The car was stolen by PAF activists and taken straight to Armagh where the co-ordinating activist garaged the vehicle.

Two weapons were also brought to Armagh for this shooting, both Smith and Wesson, one a .38 revolver, the other an automatic pistol. Two weeks prior to the original planned killing, the intended target was no longer 'available'. He had disappeared without trace, and his movements became unknown to the organisation.

In most terrorist killings, according to the PAF source, there is always a secondary target. Adrian Carroll was the secondary target in this case. After all, Loyalist terrorist mentality works on the maxim, 'if you can't kill an IRA man, kill a Taig'. The contact whom I questioned in April 1990 had obviously an involvement of some capacity in those actions. He endeavoured to convince those present by his intricate knowledge of the Carroll shooting. At times our questioning hardened the contact's response and only snippets of evidence were revealed.

What leads me to a belief that this person had involvement was his intricate knowledge not of the case but of the actual Carroll shooting. He informed us that for ten days prior to Carroll's death his movements were monitored and recorded. Carroll was employed painting railings on council premises known as McCrum's Court near the centre of Armagh, which is about ten minutes walk from his home in Abbey Street. His working hours were as regular as clockwork. The contact revealed that Adrian Carroll wore a black tracksuit with orange stripes down each arm and leg. On the day he was murdered he also wore a black donkey jacket. The contact further revealed that on 8 November Carroll was stalked for only a short distance. This corroborates the testimony of George Darling, a workmate of Adrian Carroll, who on 8 November followed a short distance (20 yards) behind Carroll as they walked along English Street towards his home.[3] Carroll was followed from the bottom of the post office where the gunman had been waiting for him. Here he could wait for his victim without arousing suspicion. He followed him up the narrow entry of Abbey Street. Elaine Faulkner's testimony corroborates this version. The man brushed past her at the bottom of Abbey Street. He was of small build, only 5′ 2″, blonde hair, a moustache, he had a small narrow face and wore gold rimmed glasses, a checked cap and a blue duffle coat.[4]

As he approached the entry Elaine Faulkner froze, as she saw him pull from his pocket a long barrelled gun. Moments later she heard the shots that killed Adrian

Carroll. The gun Elaine Faulkner saw was the .38 Smith and Wesson revolver. The other weapon was not directly used in the murder but retained by the driver of the getaway car, in case his cover was blown. The RUC forensic scientists have confirmed the calibre and make of the weapon used. The contact confirmed that the weapon was returned to its Belfast source where it has remained undetected by the RUC. One of the guns is actually still doing the rounds. In a written parliamentary answer, Mr J. Cope, the Minister for State for Northern Ireland, confirmed that the gun was never recovered, and that any ballistics from other PAF killings did not match those of the Carroll shooting.[5] However, the RUC have only run limited tests on weapons and the contact confirmed that the weapon used to kill Carroll had been in use the year before and subsequently in more recent attacks.

Elaine Faulkner's statement went on to say that she did not see the gunman after the shooting and he certainly did not pass by her as she came up Abbey Street. This backs up the testimony of Mrs Marie Hegan, the neighbour of Adrian Carroll. She lived at 12 Abbey Street. Her doorway was in the entry next to number 13 where the Carrolls lived, while her windows face Abbey Street. Her young daughter was playing in the entry when Mrs Hegan heard the shots, which were very close, the noise of them accentuated by the small alleyway in which they were fired. Mrs Hegan became distressed as she knew her daughter was outside and she could hear her child screaming and crying. She ran to the door to get her. In her statement she told the police:

> I then went into my living room where my son and the young boy Lucas were watching the television ... and within minutes I heard the sound of two distinct shots which appeared to come from some short distance away ... I went straight to the front door leaving the boys in the living room ... As I opened the door I heard a scuffling noise outside as if somebody was running up the street ...[6]

When Mrs Hegan got to her door she could only see her daughter. Another woman was heard screaming, other neighbours were gathered around Adrian Carroll. Mrs Hegan was positive she heard a running, scuffling noise going up the street towards Dawson Street. The PAF contact confirmed that the gunman made his getaway up Abbey Street where he ran to Dawson Street to the waiting stolen car.

From Dawson Street the dark blue Ford Cortina sped away to Cathedral Close. It was abandoned a short distance away. The use of the car is established by another eye-witness, James Allen. Mr Allen claimed that he heard two shots coming from the direction of Abbey Street. A short time afterwards a car went past and 'it seemed to be travelling quite fast'. Mr Allen positively identified the colour and make and the direction from which it came. He also claimed there were two people in the front of the car. He could only say the passenger was looking towards the driver. Mr Allen reported what he had seen to the police and they took a statement from him.

The car was dumped at Market Street where the men were met by another vehicle and they made their getaway to Belfast. The contact described how the number plates in the Cortina were replaced with false plates. The fixing plate was redrilled to match the holes on the false plates. This is vital material that only those involved in the planning of the murder could be aware of and would be confirmed by forensic tests on the vehicle. Tests which the police have delayed in releasing to the four men's solicitors despite repeated demands.

The contact would not confirm the number of those involved in this 'hit'. There was a gunman and driver but it appears the cell used consisted of at least two other informers and another driver. He confirmed that at no time were any UDR men involved, nor any of their families. 'The courts and judicial system along with a police force have made a significant blunder '. The gunman was free and living in Belfast without suspicion.

It was arranged that the PAF would respond to a statement to be issued by our committee calling for information on the killing. Before we parted company it was explained that the weapon used in the killing could be released for forensic testing in order to establish the authenticity of the claims that the PAF retained the murder weapon. However since the interview difficulties have emerged that have prevented a further meeting with the contact or the turning over of the weapon. In Latimer's statements he claimed the gun was dumped in the river at Portadown, subsequent searches of which recovered nothing.

I issued a statement a week later calling on the perpetrators of this evil to admit responsibility for their actions. The response from the PAF was as follows:

> We, the Protestant Action Force in a hitherto unprecedented step having been approached by concerned people with reference to recent Appeal Court decision, wish to state that the four UDR soldiers convicted of the murder of well-known Republican Adrian Carroll have not and never had any connection whatsoever with this organisation.
>
> None of these men had any prior or subsequent knowledge of events concerning the assassination of Adrian Carroll.
>
> The operation was, throughout its entirety, carried out using volunteers of the PAF and was later claimed by this organisation using properly authenticated code words.
>
> The security of our volunteers must take precedence over all else, this being the case, we unfortunately cannot point out certain discrepancies in the evidence against the convicted men ...
>
> Whilst we realise this statement will be totally inadequate in trying to right a gross miscarriage of justice, we can only hope it may help to ease some of the distress being suffered by their families and friends.
>
> We must point out that we feel the ultimate responsibility for the plight of these men lies, not with us, but with a system that can allow 4 innocent men to be coerced into

admitting to an offence they did not commit.[7]

The statement clearly covered some of the areas of discussion that evening. It later emerged that the information the PAF used to pinpoint Republican targets came from a stolen security file in which Adrian Carroll was mentioned. The police will not comment on security issues and will not confirm this information.

In a follow-up statement to a Belfast news agency, the PAF said:

> We refuse to betray our own members. We will not countenance the same sort of dishonourable conduct shown by the IRA over the Birmingham Six case when they allowed names of the allegedly real Birmingham killers to be published. The UDR men inside had nothing to do with the Carroll operation. But we will not take the ultimate step of handing over our own men to prove their innocence.[8]

In an effort to establish the possibility of this alternative, a visit to Armagh to examine the two routes became necessary.

On 12 April 1990 the same group along with Unionist MP Ken Maginnis set out for Armagh. We examined three claims. Firstly, the claims of the four convicted and their movements that day. Nine other men who were in this thirteen man patrol confirmed those movements. On 8 November 1983 the men were detailed around 13.00 hours to search an area where the RUC had seen IRA suspects the evening before. They had initially believed they were to be on a street patrol. Four landrovers were checked out and they drove to the Moy Road where two rummage searches were made lasting until 4.26 pm when Sergeant Roleston, because a mist was creating visibility difficulties, ordered his men to return to the vehicles. A long route back to the Newry Road Station brought them in just after 4.30. A fourteenth man, from an entirely different unit, Sergeant

Lowry, a UDR guard on duty at Scotch Street barrier, saw the four landrover patrols return together. Their early return was remarked upon by a sergeant major.[9] The patrol was then instructed to do vehicle checks on the main Portadown Road, looking for suspects after the shooting.

This version of events is corroborated by the four men charged, the remaining nine men of the patrol and the fourteenth man on guard duty, and the sergeant major. Two other men, who were driving along the Moy Road, recognised Corporal Hegan – the time they saw him corresponds with the time he claims to have been on that road.

The other version is the crown scenario already dealt with in detail. It alleges collusion of the security forces on a grand scale. Thirteen men all involved, four of them confessed, yet the planner remains free. They envisaged a charade of a false arrest, trips around the Mall by a break-off unit from the patrol. Several gaping holes in this version are obvious. In my view the only evidence is beyond belief and discredited by the witness' state of mind. With the hub of this story defaced beyond belief, the alleged confessions crumble on their faulty framework. The conviction is undermined by allegations made at the trial that the statements were not made voluntarily. Though the trial judge did not accept this in the case of the UDR Four he said in the case of Colin Worton that 'in the exercise of my discretion I rule his confession to be inadmissible ... there was no other evidence to maintain a case against him he was discharged'. Other critical factors just do not fit in with the crown proposition. Latimer could not have stalked Carroll and returned to College Street as quickly as was allegedly claimed in his statements. The landrover could not have completed the round trip from Lonsdale Street, the Mall, College Street and back to Newry Road by the times given.

Apart from its apparent implausibility the official scenario fails to account for certain aspects of the case. It cannot explain the role played by the Cortina car. Nor can it explain the eye-witness accounts given by Elaine Faulkner who said it definitely was not Neil Latimer. Nor can it explain why thirteen UDR soldiers would involve themselves in such a gigantic risk operation. On this basis, the judge's decision to convict upon such flimsy evidence must now be called into question.

The second scenario that the PAF contact gave offers a more realistic explanation of the Carroll killing. This explanation and the evidence produced jell better as an explanation than that tendered by the prosecution. It goes further than simply offering an alternative by dovetailing neatly with the actual UDR duties on the day in question. Despite the fact that the PAF refuse to name the killer, their story seems like a truthful answer to the riddle of the Armagh Four conviction, and once again arouses the reasonable doubt aspect over the case. If the murder is openly claimed by a terrorist organisation why then are four men claiming innocence still incarcerated for that same murder? The PAF have obviously avoided the nemesis of their actions. The police and the courts now have a duty to re-open the case and examine this alternative.

Conclusion

On 19 February 1987 Sergeant Walter Roleston was discharged from full-time UDR service. Roleston had not requested this discharge, neither could he refuse it. A finger of guilt had been wrongly pointed at him since his arrest in 1983 in connection with the Adrian Carroll murder. Roleston's military conduct was 'exemplary'. His C/O wrote on his discharge papers:

> He has served the UDR loyally for about 3 years as a Part Timer, and 12 years as a member of the Permanent Cadre. He is an efficient and trustworthy individual.

Yet this individual has found it difficult to settle down to civilian life. Not because of a personal unwillingness to do so, but due to the legacy of the finger of guilt that was pointed at him. Unlike his colleagues, who have been the subject of this book, he is free in body but remains accused and bewildered by the whole affair. The legacy of this conviction has extended further than the court's judgment. The shortcomings of the trial are many, the conclusive factors simple and straightforward. Four men have been found guilty, but upon what basis?

There is no forensic or circumstantial evidence which can be used to convict in any way. There are four confessions, yes, but similar to the statement of Witness A which has been shown to been unreliable in a number of aspects. There is identity evidence given by Witness A which has been contradicted by the identity evidence given by Elaine Faulkner. All men had alibis supported by many other soldiers, and civilian witnesses. Continual allegations that the four accused were subjected to intense mental pressure to the extent that statements were not voluntarily given has given rise to doubts as to whether they should have been admitted as evidence against them. The crown's chief witness has accused the police of tricks and has continually claimed that Latimer was no murderer. That same witness, both during and since the trial, has discredited her own testimony to a point where it can no longer be deemed acceptable. The other chief eye-witness is positive the gunman she saw was 'definitely not Latimer'.

The only evidence is uncorroborated evidence. In Scotland uncorroborated evidence which convicted three of the men would have been insufficient to have merited a conviction. Considering that evidence presented was riddled with inconsistencies and was not corroborated the case demands an immediate and independent enquiry. During seven years of incarceration and accusation, each man has unswervingly denied guilt. The police have stated that 'substantial reasons exist in this particular case for a review of some of the evidence'. A terrorist organisation not only admitted responsibility, but has outlined in detail how and why the murder was committed. No jury has heard this evidence. So you, the reader, are now a jury – what say you?

An ever-increasing list of people of influence and opinion-formers have added their names to the catalogue of doubt; Lord Fitt has said, 'I have only recently become aware of the circumstances of this case and I feel there could be reasonable doubts on the validity of their convictions'. Robert Kee has been even more outspoken,'I am totally convinced that the convictions of the Armagh Four are unsafe and unsatisfactory'. Ian Paisley has claimed that a 'mis-trial has occurred and that it would be unsafe in law to keep these men in prison because of the flawed nature of the evidence upon which they were convicted'. Merlyn Rees has supported the calls for an enquiry, 'the main evidence against these men arises from confessions. This, together with a retraction by a main witness, raises reasonable doubts about the sentences imposed. There should be an enquiry'. In view of the growing public concern, corrective action is an immediate necessity.

Fair and independent ESDA tests should be initiated, a retrial ordered and the convictions quashed. No political trade-off or balancing of the books is sought; simply justice and fair play for all. This interesting body of new evidence and fresh factors is waiting for an official hearing. The Secretary of State has the power to remit the case to the Court of Appeal at any time he sees fit.

For the four men, especially Hegan, time ticks by. Seeing his children grow up, and his wife, Lillian, cope with life without her husband, is difficult, to say the least. The other three men are younger and therefore have even more to live for – more dreams to fulfil and experiences to sample. All four are determined and articulate scribes. They write continually to men and women from all walks of life protesting their innocence. The future for the men at present is gloomy, destined to etch out an existence in prison. The driving motive behind the campaign has been, and remains, hope. Others like Roleston, who is condemned but un-jailed, lives in a prison of his own. No visible walls exist, no bars to peer through, but the underlying accusation that he lives with is that he too is guilty but uncharged. It has affected his life, employment and family. He does not seek revenge but awaits the day when he, like his colleagues, will be set free from the ever-present accusing finger of guilt. Lives have been overturned. Families have been tortured with stressful agony. Justice demands a retrial before time runs out.

The legacy of doubts demand that an effective policing of the police operations and interrogation procedure is put into fervent action, not in a way that will hamper the police in obtaining positive results in their difficult but necessary fight against terrorism, but in an effective manner to guard against such recurrences of doubt. Laws that have been instigated to protect human rights now appear up-rooted to retract those rights. This case illustrates the immense dangers of reliance upon uncorroborated confession evidence. To guard against such injustice an insistence upon corroboration on every count is an immediate necessity for all cases where a confession is contested. This requirement is reinforced in Northern Ireland because of the Diplock court system. Trial without a jury places an imperative upon the judge to see and hear only evidence that can be effect-ively substantiated and proved beyond a reasonable doubt. Recent curtailments upon the right to silence signal another blow to a fair and free system, which reinforces my point. Interrogations should not only be monitored, as is the present case, but videoed as Lord Colville recommended. A safeguard for the suspect and the interrogator would have to be imposed where the judge would only be permitted to view this evidence. Serious attention must also be given to the appeal mechanism. An independent and pre-trial tribunal could be established to consider such cases in full, with powers to recommend a verdict. Such demands if put into operation could, in effect, alter the face of the British legal system. But then, if such serious doubts can appear can Britain and Northern Ireland afford not to take corrective action? Such renovations to the system are long overdue.

The ultimate deciding factor in this case which a senior-ranking army officer maintains is that 'if such irregular activities had taken place serious questions would have been asked'. That statement guarantees that the checks and balances in the UDR camp on 8 November 1983 were adequate and sufficient to undermine significantly any illegal activity that could have been planned. It is time for this mutilation of justice to be put right. The police and courts must now produce the answers.

POSTSCRIPT

On 3 January 1991 the long awaited reply from the RUC with regard to the ESDA tests was at last received. This reply was provoked by a parliamentary question asked just before parliament rose for the Christmas break.

> Dr Paisley: To ask the Secretary of State for Northern Ireland, what are the reasons for the delay in the report on ESDA tests on the evidence relating to the case relating to four members of the UDR from Armagh, and ordered by Chief Constable on 31 July.

Dr Brian Mawhinney replied on 19 December:

> The report has been delayed by the need to subject a large volume of material to detailed and thorough examination; but I understand that the work is now virtually complete and that the NIFSL expect to be able to submit their findings to the RUC shortly.

Since this riposte events, that for some time appeared to be caught up in bureaucratic red tape, unfolded at a steady pace. This parliamentary answer was indicative of what news I was to receive on 3 January from the RUC. For five months the authorities had refused the men's solicitors access to the material that was subject to the tests. Anxiety surrounding what the scientists were actually doing had been expressed by the solicitors who have been shamefully kept in the dark about the identity of the actual documents that are being tested. Late that afternoon the Chief Constable released the following statement:

> A preliminary forensic science report on ESDA tests of RUC interview notes in respect of the UDR four has now been

138

received by the RUC. As a result of this preliminary report certain points require further clarification/investigation and the Chief Constable has appointed a senior officer, a Detective Chief Superintendent from RUC Headquarters to make further enquiries into this matter.

Dissecting this statement certain aspects must be highlighted. Firstly this was not the much elusive and long-awaited report promised since July, but rather an assurance that a preliminary report had been made. It is believed the contents of this preliminary report suggest that serious inconsistencies in the police papers tested have shown up and as a result of their seriousness the RUC feel a full investigation must be held. Secondly the appointment of a senior officer from Headquarter's staff demonstrates the seriousness in which the Chief Constable is viewing this case in light of the report. It demonstrates that Hugh Annesley is at pains to keep his eye on developments. Thirdly if there were no, or simply minor, inconsistencies found in the papers the RUC would have made public their report some time ago and diminished claims that the UDR Four are innocent.

The RUC report will undoubtedly take some time to complete. However police authority and forensic science contacts suggest that it is not an exaggeration to say that the content of the preliminary report is fantastic. So far, five hundred documents consisting of between two and five pages each, have been subjected to ESDA tests. It is understood in reliable sources that these have shown up a number of inconsistencies that require explanation. For many this revelation has vindicated a campaign for a retrial. Another pillar of the crown case has crumbled to the foundations. I believe we are standing on the verge of a judicial tidal wave that will have repercussions beyond the narrow scope of this case. These repercussions will be significantly greater than any other case in Northern Ireland and arguably British judicial history.

The solicitors acting for the men remain anxious that the RUC enquiry could drag its heels on this investigation and final report, and thus impede the speedy solution to this case. At a meeting with the Secretary of State in London, one week after the police statement, the seriousness of the case was endorsed by Peter Brooke, who expressed the view that the matter deserved a thorough examination. He indicated that he would endeavour to look at the case with expedition. A dossier containing new evidence has been given to him. This evidence includes all of the above and two other pieces of new evidence.

On the one hand the credibility of Witness A as a reliable witness has once again been scrutinised. (See Hansard Report of Parliamentary Debate on the UDR Four, 6 March 1991.)

BBC Newsnight in a documentary have released information that has significant bearing on the confession evidence. A technique known as syntax analysis or word patterns has been developed and perfected by Dr Andrew Q. Morton, a Fellow of the Royal Society of Edinburgh. Morton contends that everyone has an individual pattern of speech and writing as distinctive as a fingerprint. He independently examined certain documents in relation to this case. In a report Morton suggests that the statements produced in court as being one man's confession were wrong and some had as many as three separate authors. Dr Morton goes further and states that, 'Not one of them is a genuine confession of the accused'. It is my contention that such a claim should be heard in court and Dr Morton has said that he would be prepared to take this evidence to a court.

The ESDA tests go to the foundation of this case because they examine the police interview notes and will determine if they are a cogent, clear and accurate reflection of what was said by these men during their interrogation. The syntax tests examine the actual alleged confessions and determine who is their author. On both counts there are reasonable doubts concerning the evidence upon which these men were convicted.

The nature of this case demands that the countdown to these men's freedom is begun in earnest.

Chronology of Events

1981: Latimer meets Witness A at factory.

1979-1983: Hegan, Bell, Latimer and Allen join full-time UDR.

12 December 1982: Séamus Grew and Roddy Carroll shot dead by RUC. Enquiry into RUC shoot to kill policy demanded.

September 1983: PAF plan killing of IRA target in Armagh.

8 September 1983: Veronica Truesdale's car stolen from Shankill Road and taken to Armagh.

30 October 1983: PAF target IRA man in Armagh, then claim he disappeared and Adrian Carroll chosen as secondary target.

2 November 1983: Winston Allen joins D company.

7 November 1983: RUC spot suspect terrorists in Moy Road area of Armagh. Request UDR to search this area.

8 November 1983: *12 o'clock:* 13 UDR soldiers including Roleston, Allen, Hegan, Bell, Latimer, Worton, sent to carry out search following RUC request.

1 o'clock: Search begins.
4.20: Witness A claims to be in Lonsdale Street.

4.26: Roleston calls off search – prosecution claim he left earlier.

4.30-4.35: Elaine Faulkner sees gunman in Abbey Street.

4.35: Carroll shot in Abbey Street. Mrs Marie Hegan hears gunman running away. James Allen sees car speeding away from vicinity of shooting. Constable Williamson hears shots and drives to Abbey Street.

4.36: Four landrovers arrive back at base. Sgt Lowry, on duty at Scotch Street, sees landrovers return. Sgt Major retasks the soldiers to a VCP on the Belfast/Portadown Road.

4.55: Elaine Faulkner supplies police with statement.

7.30: Carroll dies in hospital. PAF admit responsibility.

9 November 1983: RUC, having found the abandoned Cortina car, begin enquiries into crime.

Dates Unknown: Witness A meets with Fr Faul and Fr Murray and accuses Latimer of some involvement in the mock-arrest.

29 November 1983: Latimer arrested and questioned by the police in Castlereagh.

2 December 1983: Formalised statement from Witness A given to RUC.

29 November – 6 December 1983: After interrogations and confrontations Latimer, Bell, Hegan, Allen and Worton sign statements. All allege duress and claim mistreatment. (All remanded in custody.)

24 May 1984: Stalker enquiry into shoot to kill begins.

3 March – 1 July 1986: Trial of UDR Four.

1 July 1986: Guilty verdict (Appeal Court upheld decision).

5 February 1989: Witness A accuses police of tricks.

31 July 1990: Permission for ESDA granted to the UDR Four.

January 1991: Dossier of new evidence presented to the Secretary of State – awaiting his reply.

Appendix

Statement
from Norman and Margaret Bell on meeting with Fr Faul

Máiréad Maguire, famous for her work in the Peace Movement has taken great interest in the case of the Armagh Four since Noel Bell began to write to her some months ago. Since visiting Noel in prison and hearing the many worrying aspects of the case Máiréad is now completely convinced that a great miscarriage of justice exists in this case.

Due to the part played by Fr Faul and Fr Murray she decided to telephone Fr Faul in order to clarify a few points regarding his involvement. In the course of this telephone conversation on 11 June 1990, Fr Faul revealed certain information which Máiréad felt should be made available to us, Noel Bell's parents. An immediate meeting was arranged to take place at midday between Fr Faul, Máiréad and ourselves.

At our meeting the case was discussed at length with Fr Faul insisting that Neil Latimer was the gunman, however, he admitted that his only reason for believing this was because of the statement made to him and Fr Murray by Witness A whom he described as a simple honest Catholic woman.

Towards the end of our meeting Máiréad asked Fr Faul if he would explain to us certain events which took place prior to the arrest of the UDR soldiers and which he had outlined to her earlier that day. At this point Fr Faul appeared to be rather perturbed but due to Máiréad's insistence he described both his and Fr Murray's involvement as follows.

After being contacted by Witness A they sought a meeting with a local senior police officer in Armagh who, after having heard allegations that UDR soldiers were alleged to have been involved in the murder of Adrian Carroll, commented: 'I hope that this is not true'. This comment caused the priests some concern as they felt that there was a possibility of this matter being 'brushed under the carpet'. Therefore they decided to consult someone in higher authority, and in Fr Faul's own words: 'The Chief Constable and Higher'.

It was agreed at this meeting that before a statement was given to the RUC certain conditions would have to be met and are listed below:

> 1: That an entire UDR patrol, operating in the north of the city, should be arrested by police officers from another locality.
> 2: That the UDR soldiers should be taken to a holding centre other than Gough Barracks, namely Castlereagh.
> 3: Interrogating officers should be of senior rank and again the majority of these officers preferably completely unknown to any of the soldiers ...

[Fr Faul has described this accusation as fiction. In an article by John Devine in the Sunday Independent *on 17 February 1991 he denies all the allegations made by Nobel peace prize-winner Máiréad Maguire and the Bells. He also rejects that he spoke to Sir John Hermon. Sir John Hermon confirms this in the same article – he said: 'With regard to the apparent suggestion in the documents submitted to the Secretary of State that I met Fr Faul in relation to the so-called 'Armagh Four', I state categorically that there is no substance or truth in that statement.*

'I have never had any such meeting with any of these

people, or with any other people concerning this matter.']

... A second meeting between Máiréad Maguire, Fr Faul and ourselves took place on 13 July 1990, when following general discussions we returned to the subject of the priest's involvement in this case. Máiréad made a request asking if Fr Faul would consider making a public statement regarding both his and Fr Murray's involvement and the requests made to higher authority ensuring that the UDR soldiers would be arrested and interrogated as stipulated by them.

He promised to consider this request but felt that to make a public statement could present some difficulties, he did not elaborate further. Numerous approaches have been made to him since 31 July 1990, by Máiréad but to date no such statement has been forthcoming.

Finally the blunt refusal by Fr Murray to meet us and discuss the case gives us further cause for concern.

Norman and Margaret Bell
17 October 1990

Glossary of Terms Used

RUC	Royal Ulster Constabulary
UDR	Ulster Defence Regiment
UVF	Ulster Volunteer Force
PAF	Protestant Action Force
IRA	Irish Republican Army
INLA	Irish National Liberation Army
HQMSU	Head Quarters Mobile Support Unit
VCP	Vehicle Check Point
OC	Officer in Command
DPP	Department of Public Prosecutions
OPs	Operation
Pte	Private
Sgt	Sergeant
SIB	Special Investigation Bureau

NOTES

Chapter 2

1. Interview, Mrs Latimer, May 1990.
2. High court judgment, 1 July 1986, pp. 14–15.
3. *Ibid.*, pp. 15–16.
4. *Ibid.*, pp. 19–22.
5. *Ibid.*, p. 22.
6. *Ibid.*, p. 22–23.
7. *Ibid.*, p.23; p. 44.
8. Latimer Interview, Maghaberry, February 1990.
9. High court judgment, 1 July 1986, p. 81–82.
10. James Hegan interview, February 1990.
11. High court judgment, 1 July 1986, pp. 90–91.
12. *Ibid.*, pp. 91–93.
13. Trial papers, Dr L Burton, 8 April 1986, pp. 19–23.
14. Trial papers, 18 March 1986, p. 38.
15. *Ibid.*, 18 March 1986, p. 56.
16. *Ibid.*, p. 56–58.
17. *Ibid.*, p. 59.
18. *Ibid.*, p. 52a.
19. *Ibid.*, p. 59.
20. High court judgment, 1 July 1986, p. 62
21. *Ibid.*, pp. 62 – 64.
22. *Ibid.*, p. 76.
23. *Ibid.*, p. 76.
24. *Ibid.*, p. 3 – 4.
25. *Voir Dire*, trial papers, 20 May 1986, p. 65.
26. *Ibid.*, 20 May 1986, p. 55, 56.
27. *Ibid.*, 20 May 1986, p. 56.
28. *Ibid.*, 20 May 1986, p. 70.
29. High court judgment, 1 July 1986, pp. 121–122
30. *Ibid.*, p. 122–123.
31. *Ibid.*, p. 127.
32. *Ibid.*, p. 134.
33. *Ibid.*, p. 22 – 33; 62 – 64; 91 – 93.
34. H. Skillen, letter, June 1990.
35. *News Letter,* 5 June 1990.
36. *Time Bomb*, McKee and Franey (Foreword).

Chapter 3

1. *Irish News*, 8 December 1983.
2. *Ibid*.
3. *Belfast Telegraph*, 12 December 1983.
4. Government statistics from parliamentary question.
5. An enquiry into alleged RUC cover-ups of anti-terrorist activities 1982-1983
6. Sinn Féin/Danny Morrison election slogan, 1982.
7. BBC Panorama, 20 February 1990.
8. Parliamentary written question.
9 John Hume, addressing party conference, November 1988.
10. *Irish News*, 5 December 1983.
11. Sir John Hermon, *Chief Constable's Report, 1984*, p. 15–16.
12. Bell statement, 17 October 1990.
13. *Sunday Independent*, 17 February 1991.
14. *Belfast Telegraph*, 9 November 1983.
15. Statement, Elaine Faulkner, 8 November 1983.
16. *Ibid*.
17. *Ibid*.
18. Letter to RUC, 3 May 1990; Letter from RUC 18 May 1990.
19. House of Commons question 85.
20. Statement, Witness A.
21. High court judgment, 1 July 1986, p 2.
22. *Ibid.*, p. 2.
23. *Ibid.*, p. 6.
24. Trial papers, 5 March 1986, p. 66.
25. *Ibid.*, 11 March 1986, p. 35–37.
26. High court judgment, 1 July 1986, p 11.
27. *Irish News*, 2 July 1986.
28. *Ibid*.
29. High court judgment, 1 July 1986, p 43.

Chapter 4

1. Letter from James Hegan to Dr Ian Paisley, 23 October 1989.
2. High court judgment, 1 July 1986, p. 2.
3. Roleston interview, April 1990
4. *Ibid*.
5. Letter, 23 October 1989 from J Hegan to Dr Paisley.
6. Trial papers, 9 June 1986, p. 17.
7. RTE, 5 February 1989.
8. Witness A's statement.

9. Trial papers, 11 March 1986,1896, p. 63.
10. Trial papers, 18 June 1986, p. 36 – 37.
11. Dossier, para 96–100.
12. Witness statement, retained as new evidence.
13. Statement, James Allen.
14. Letter to RUC, 3 May 1990.
15. Letter from RUC, 18 May 1990.
16. High court judgment, 1 July 1986, p. 10.
17. RTE, 5 February 1989.

Chapter 5

1. Letter from Ian Stewart, 24 July 1989.
2. Exhibit 7, 29 November 1983.
3. Exhibit 9, 2 December 1983.
4. Trial papers, 3 March 1986, p. 24; High court judgment, 1 July 1986, p. 1.
5. Exhibit 7, 29 November 1983.
6. Exhibit 9, 2 December 1983.
7. High court judgment, 1 July 1986, p. 28.
8. *Irish News*, 4 December 1990.
9. Trial papers, 9 June 1986, p. 34.
10. *Ibid.*, p. 36.
11. *Ibid.*, p. 36.
12. *Ibid.*, p. 38.
13. *Ibid.*, p. 38.
14. High court judgment, 1 July 1986, p. 22.
15. *Ibid.*, p. 22.
16. RTE, 5 February 1989.
17. *Voir Dire*, 18 March 1986, p. 52a.
18. *Ibid.*, p. 54–59.
19. *Ibid.*, p. 36.
20. Lord Lane, 19 October 1989
21. *Voir Dire*, 22 April 1986, p. 55–58.
22. *Ibid.*, p. 58–60.
23. Letter from RUC, 31 July 1990.
24. High court judgment, 1 July 1986, pp. 101, 102, 105, 108.
25. *Ibid.*, p. 83.
26. Trial papers, 7 May 1986, pp. 11, 13.
27. *Voir Dire*, 7 May 1986, p. 23.
28. *Ibid.*, p. 25.
29. High court judgment, 1 July 1986, p. 85–87.
30. High court judgment, 1 July 1986, p. 88.
31. Taylor's Letter, 21 March 1990.

32. High court judgment, p. 119.
33. *Ibid.*, p. 122.
34. Taylor's letter, 21 March 1990.
35. *Ibid.*
36. Trial papers, 20 May 1986, p.78–81.

Chapter 6

1. High court judgment, 1 July 1986, p 5.
2. *Ibid.*, p. 5.
3. *Ibid.*, p. 31–32.
4. *Ibid.*, p. 35.
5. Trial papers, 5 March 1986, p. 52.
6. Statement, 2 December 1983.
7. *Ibid.*
8. *Ibid.*
9. *Ibid.*
10. *Ibid.*
11. *Ibid.*
12. *Ibid.*
13. *Ibid.*
14. *Ibid.*
15. Trial papers, 5 March 1986, p. 66–73.
16. *Ibid.*, p. 62–65.
17. *Ibid.*, p. 64.
18. High court judgment, 1 July 1986, p. 5.
19. *Ibid.*, p .2;4.
20. Trial papers, 5 March 1986, p. 52–60.
21. *Ibid.*, 11 March 1986, p. 35 –38.
22. *Ibid.*, 10 March 1986, p. 58 –60.
23. *Ibid.*, 101March 1986, p. 25.
24. *Ibid.*,10 March 1986, p. 66.
25. *Ibid.*, 5 March 1986, p. 52.
26. *Ibid.*, 11 March 1986, p. 1.
27. *Ibid.*, p. 60.
28. RTE, 5 February 1989.
29. Trial papers, 5 March 1986, p. 54.
30. *Ibid.*, 10 March 1986, p. 35–36.
31. *Ibid.*, p. 23.
32. *Ibid.*, p. 23–24.
33. *Ibid.*, p. 21–23.
34. *Ibid.*, 11 March 1986, p. 35–37.
35. *Ibid.*, p. 64.
36. High court judgment, 1 July 1986, p 52.

37. Trial papers, 9 June 1986, p. 5.
38. *Ibid.*, p. 6.
39. RTE, 5 February 1989; trial papers, 9 June 1986, p. 7.
40. Trial papers, 9 June 1986, p. 7.
41. Hegan tape, 17 August 1990.
42. RTÉ, 5 February 1989.
43. Letter, from T. King to Lord Mason , 3 May 1989.
44. *Ibid.*
45. Letter, from I. Stewart to P. Robinson, 24 July 1989.
46. Dossier.

Chapter 7

1. High court judgment, 1 July 1986, p. 52.
2. Trial papers, 4 March 1986, p. 68.
3. *Ibid.*, p. 59.
4. Statement, 8 November 1983.
5. House of Commons, question 85.
6. Trial papers, 4 March 1986, p. 45.
7. PAF statement.
8. *Sunday World*, 29 April 1990.
9. Witness, identity undisclosed for security.

INDEX